PEAKS

PEAKS

SEEKING HIGH GROUND
ACROSS THE CONTINENTS

▲ ▲ ▲

Richard Bangs

Photography by Pamela Roberson

TAYLOR PUBLISHING COMPANY
DALLAS, TEXAS

Also by

RICHARD BANGS

Rivergods

Islandgods

Whitewater Adventure

Riding the Dragon's Back
(WITH CHRISTIAN KALLEN)

Paths Less Travelled
(WITH CHRISTIAN KALLEN, EDITORS)

Islands of Fire, Islands of Spice
(WITH CHRISTIAN KALLEN)

The Adventure Book

1,001 Vacations

Great Adventures

Adventure Vacations
(EDITOR)

Frontispiece: Torres del Paine, Patagonia
Page iii: Annapurna, Nepal; Southern Alps, New Zealand
Page vi: Mount Cook, New Zealand

Published by Taylor Publishing Company
1550 West Mockingbird Lane
Dallas, Texas 75235

Designed by David Timmons

Library of Congress Cataloging-in-Publication Data

Bangs, Richard, 1950–
    Peaks : seeking the high ground across the continents / Richard Bangs ;
    photography by Pamela Roberson.
            p.   cm.
    ISBN 0-87833-856-X
    I. Mountains.   I. Title.
    GB501.2.B36   1994
910'.02143—dc20   94-19196
                                                                       CIP

10   9   8   7   6   5   4   3   2   1

Printed in the United States of America

CONTENTS

He who makes the true ascent must ascend
forever.

—Saint Gregory of Nyssa

PREFACE

It began with a vision.

Mount Vision, nothing more than a nub on the global face, is a place where the world seems to unfurl an infinite cloth, and the sun sets with a deep, fiery orange—the color of creation. We had come to this seaside hill in Marin County for a simple Saturday camping holiday, a quick escape from the salt of the city. Though we didn't see a soul as we wandered around the green flanks, we did see a sign announcing that Mount Vision closed at sunset. Try as man might, Nature doesn't close, especially at sunset, so we set out to find a level spot with a view near the modest summit. Yet after darkness spread its blanket, sleep didn't come. Our dogs barked at the unheard sounds of a hundred wild creatures; and every hour or so a ranger drove by beneath us, headlights sweeping just beyond our toes. Just my luck, I cursed. Mountains have always been anathema to me, and now I would probably be arrested on one. When I was quite young, and growing up in Connecticut, I would sometimes ramble about a rock called Sleeping Giant Mountain, until one time my cousin, Jimmy, fell from a cliff. He was lost for hours, until a rescue team dragged him from a scree pile. He was bruised, lucky to be alive, and parents wagged fingers about how dangerous mountains were. I believed them. Later, when I was a river guide in the Sierras, my roommate was a fresh, free-spirited soul named Judy. One day I received a call. Judy's mountain-guide husband had died in a climbing accident, and I would have to relay the news. Telling Judy was one of the hardest things I had ever done. Mountains, I was re-notified, would not be mine.

Yet, my eyes were irremediably drawn upwards; and my reading material was often about people who seemed mythopoetic to me: Edmund Hillary, Tenzing Norgay, Maurice Herzog, Barry Bishop, George Mallory, Chris Bonington, and Reinhold Messner. I could never do what these larger-than-lifers had. I didn't have the skills, the charged physique, or the guts. The peaks of mountains would remain as dreams, there but untouchable, and wrapped in clouds, but with no texture or grain.

My life as a lowlander had worked pretty well to date. I had skirted the globe, run many rivers, sailed half a dozen seas. Yet, something arched in my soul. An inner skin was shedding. There was an unexplored landscape beckoning, a sharp place with an ever-changing interplay of shadow and light. In some preintellectual way, I needed to set out. And this time the travel would be about transformation, not transportation; about guides, not gods.

Sometime around midnight the last ranger left, and the soothing utterances of the mountain rushed in. Sleep spun its web. And, with the morning it was so clear I could see across the Pacific. I could we west to the great mountains of the east, to the Himalaya, and beyond to the Alps. It was so clear, in all directions there were the mountains of the world. And so we took the inital steps in a long journey, the first footfalls in a trek for the high ground across the continents. We found adventure; we found views; we found whorls of tranquility, storminess, sweat, and perspicacity; and we discovered things under the rocks and above the clouds that emancipated perception, and rendered previous understandings obsolete. We found wonderful things never imagined. And they are here within...

ACKNOWLEDGEMENTS

A mountain is the ultimate metaphor, and we certainly won't miss the chance to invoke a comparison. Though all lines on a mountain come to a point, a glistening pinnacle in the sun, a singular summit to which all eyes are drawn, there is an enormous support structure, an underhistory that quietly builds the foundation the glorious tip rests upon. So it is with a book. While a writer or photographer climbs some private artistic landscape, and pulls creative inspiration from a solo inner trek to reach a place where all the world can see the realization of efforts, there is an entire expedition of assistance, people and organizations who lend hands, belay ropes, carry loads, and hold up the flags. It takes an entire *cordillera* to produce a work such as this, and we would like to acknowledge some of those whose generous help, guidance, and support created the selection of peak experiences you now hold in your hands.

If you are going to tramp about the mountains of the world nothing is as important as footwear, and so we want to thank THE DEXTER SHOE COMPANY, which supplied the waterproof boots we wore throughout these journeys. While lesser soles caused others travelling with us to suffer, we never once developed blisters, and always had dry feet. At Dexter, we especially want to thank Peter Lunder, Dan Miller, and Susan Haviland.

These days a writer can't work without a computer, and for that we want to thank AT&T GLOBAL INFORMATION SOLUTIONS and Sean Glynn. They supplied the AT&T Safari computer, which was carried to the tops of mountains, where words were composed on the spot.

And, a photographer in the moody landscapes of mountains needs the best, most reliable camera gear. We want to thank CANON CAMERAS for the incredible Eos and the excellent lenses, many provided by the Canon CPS Loan program with David Metz and Joe Relora; THE SAUNDERS GROUP (and Marica Dlutek) for the Benbo Trekker tripod, and SLIK AMERICA for 333 Sport Tripod, both of which work anywhere, anytime. LOWEPRO USA (and David Riley) for the finest designed camera bags in the world. We especially want to thank EASTMAN KODAK and John Altberg for the lustrous film, particularly Lumiere, which is showcased throughout this work. CUSTOM PROCESS of Berkeley, California, we thank for the film processing.

We want to thank EAGLE CREEK (and Ricky Schlesinger) for the tough yet smart travel luggage we carried; LOWE ALPINE SYSTEMS for the expedition outwear and gloves used at high altitudes; THE NORTH FACE for the sleeping bags and tents; TEVA and Mark Thatcher for the sports sandals; BASIC DESIGNS for the comfortable air mattresses; TILLEY ENDURABLES for the hats; BUCK for the knives; BAUME & MERCIER (and Lisa Walborsky) for the Formula S watch that kept time no matter the temperature or terrain; BAD (Best American Duffle) for the hold-everything duffles; LEKI SPORT (and Greg Wozer) for the hiking poles that supported us on every trek; CLIMB HIGH (and Tom Nold) for the Julbo glacier glasses; EX OFFICIO for the best-designed trekking shirts in the world; TERRAMAR SPORTS WORLDWIDE for the Transport long underwear; THULE USA (and Bruce Bossidy) for the roof rack; MINOLTA cameras and lenses for Richard's photography; GOOKINAID ERG for the energy drinks; POWERBAR for the extra oomph needed to make the top; CAMPMOR for the Technical Gortex Parkas; DUOFOLD for the Thermax underwear; THE COLEMAN COMPANY for the Apex stove; GENERAL ECOLOGY for our First Need water-filter system; and REEF BRAZIL for our camp sandals.

Getting to and around each mountain was a monumental task, and many helped to ease the passage. They include:

MONT BLANC: Swiss Air and Ron Kuhlmann; The Swiss National Tourist Office and Joe Lustenberger and Daniel Bacher; Bernard Prud'Homme of the Chamonix Office du Tourisme; Eve Peterson, the French Alps Commission; Eric Glattfelder and the Hotel du Rhone; Danny and Jon Morris; Nichole Peelle; and Susan Pritchard who helped with the French translations.

KILIMANJARO: British Airways and Jill Donaldson; Wes Krause, Dana Adler, Allen Bechky, Christine Furnas, William Broyles Jr., Bob Finney, Carl Schenker and Susan Richardson, Lee Meyers, Dr. Stephen Levine, Nairobi's Norfolk Hotel, The Crater Lodge, Mt. Meru Game Lodge, The Dik Dik Hotel, Dr. Charles Wilson, Dr. Cliff Roberson, and Daniel, our lead mountain guide.

TAAL AND PINATUBO: Philippine Airlines; Maria Elena (Peachy) Villanueva and

ACKNOWLEDGEMENTS

the Philippine Department of Tourism; Puerto Azul Beach Resort; The Manila Hotel; Narzalina Lim of the Asia Pacific Tourism Development Corp.; Tita Romero; Remedios Raymundo; Daniel Corpuz; Georgina Monsod; Betty Nelle; Vic Milan of Conservation International; and Leslie Jarvie.

MOUNT CHANCE: American Airlines and Richard Zachman; Mike Fagin; Veronica Stoddard; Dr. Dean and Undine Burget; The Montserrat Foundation; Pace Advertising; Governor David Taylor; Hickson's Taxi & Tours; The Blue Dolphin; Montserrat Airways; The Vue Pointe Hotel; Belham Valley Restaurant; The Nest; Captain Martine Haxby; Rose Willock of Radio Montserrat; and Perks Liqueur.

MOUNT COOK: United Airlines and Peter Cosovich and Michael Ricco; David Hicks of the Open Polytechnic of New Zealand; PATA; David Beattie; A.C. Staniford; The Mount Cook Group and Prue Norling; Alpine Guides and Bryan Carter; The Hermitage Hotel; Sir Edmund Hillary; John Woods of *Adventure* magazine; Norbu Tenzing Norgay; and Mary Gerber of Executive Outdoor Adventures.

MOUNT RAINIER: Leo LeBon, who kindly lent his climbing boots, crampons and ice ax; Chuck Cross who helped fit them; friends Tom Peirce, Dave Shore, Howard Brainen, Steve Marks, and Gary Beck, who joined the climb.

TIEN SHAN MOUNTAINS: Finnair and Kirsti Maki; Aeroflot; Charlie Ross; John Yost; Misha Harshan and his Soviet Travels for Peace and the Environment; Project RAFT; fellow explorers Vanja Maurakh, Sergey Kirillov, Kirby Ellis, Jana Janus, Joe Kaminsky, Alfred Syachelna, Dominic Mubika, Ludmila Linvova, Tonya Shaligina, Steve Gilroy, and Sharon Ahern; and the Harkush rapids.

ANNAPURNA: Thai Airways International and Serm Phenjati; the marvelous Mo Decoursey; The Hotel Malla and the Malla family; Malla Treks and Stan Armington; Narendra Gurung; Lisa Fisher; and fellow trekkers Steph Lieberman, Kathleen Whitby, Patricia Papa, and the Blackburn family.

ATLAS MOUNTAINS: Royal Air Maroc and Hanine Arous; Atlas Sahara Trek and Brahim Errachiki; Ambassador Peter and Harvel Sebastian; Mohamed Hakki; Barry Brukoff; Eva Harris; Etoile du Toubkal; and Paul Bowles.

TORRES DEL PAINE: Ladeco Chilean Airlines and our good and longtime friend, Diana Samper; the explora, en Patagonia lodge; The Carerra Hotel, Santiago; and Sheraton Hotels.

We'd also like to thank the following: friend and advisor Hap Klopp; George and Diane Fuller; Jeff Blumenfeld of Blumenfeld and Associates; Pat and Jack Brickhouse of Channel Marketing; Fred Khrehbiel and Tom Lee of Molex; Tom McCormack; Harold Knutson for his advice and bottomless research materials; Linda Mariaca and Mia Pearson for pet- and house-sitting; Russ Daggatt, Dave Parker, Dick McGowan, Dena Bartolome, Jim Ahern, Nadia LeBon, who held down the fort; Kathryn Winogura, Gretchen Hamberg, and Liz Longstreth who did the same; Richard Deacon of Sobek Canada; Leslie Stoval who supplied the music for inspiration; Geoff Berggren; and Julie Atherton.

Yes, our parents deserve great credit for supporting our wanderings, Dr. Lawrence and Louise Bangs, and Frank Roberson.

And, the good people at TAYLOR PUBLISHING, including publisher Lynn Brooks, marketing wiz Jim Green, former editor Jim Donovan, and our current editor Lorena Jones.

Last, we want to thank MOUNTAIN TRAVEL•SOBEK, THE ADVENTURE COMPANY, upon whose trips many of these words and pictures were created.

Logic and time were kidnapped and made this possible.
And so we dedicate this book, with love, to b.B.

CASCADES

Mt.Rainier ○

○ Mt.Chance

CARIBBEAN

A Tour of the World's Great Mountains

Torres del Paine ○ PATAGONIA

THE ALPS
○ Mont Blanc

CENTRAL ASIA

Tien Shan Mountains

The Atlas
ATH AFRICA

HIMALAYAS
Annapurna ○

Mt. Taal &
○ Mt. Pinatubo

EAST AFRICA

MALAY ARCHIPELAGO

○ Kilimanjaro

Mt. Batur ○

Mt. Cook ○

NEW ZEALAND

Those who are wise or think they are, aimlessly repeat that it is madness to face such fatigue, to risk one's life to visit those deserts; a mysterious attraction draws us there and there are always men to undertake such pilgrimages towards the unknown. Many of them do it again and again, in spite of danger, fatigue, hunger or thirst. It is a passion similar to gambling.

—VIOLLET-LE-DUC, 1870

MONT BLANC:
THE GUIDES MUST
BE CRAZY

The precise meaning of this exercise escapes me. I'm in a world of white, inching up a knife-edge ridge that plunges 1,000 feet in one direction, 9,000 feet in the other. Does it matter which way I fall? I must resemble an ant negotiating the tractionless rim of a bathtub. My head is a bit dizzy, my breathing sharp, and my senses mentholated from the vistas. But I'm okay, I keep reassuring myself. Then as I take a step my right crampon snags my baggy left trouser leg and rips the inseam. For a second I lose balance and blood rushes to my head. Grabbing some composure, I continue the climb. I'm too frightened to take my eyes off my feet, but when we stop to rest I allow an upward glance. Just three miles ahead looms a gleaming white whale breaching a sea of ice, the 15,771-foot-high peak of Mont Blanc. This is the mountain that has claimed the lives of more climbers than any other peak in the world, over two thousand to date. I know there is a view of the Matterhorn directly behind me, but I don't dare take a look.

A few steps later the crampon again bites into my pants and catches, and I start to drop into space. The rope goes taut; I collapse onto my knees and instinctively bury the wrong end of the ice ax into the snow. I'm sprawled, spread-eagled, over this arête, panting and terrified. But Serge turns to me and says in a thickly accented,

THE VIEW FROM THE REFUGE DES COSMIQUES. AT 11,583 FEET, IT IS ONE OF THE HIGHEST HOTELS IN THE WORLD AND CAN ONLY BE REACHED BY DONNING CRAMPONS AND CLIMBING A GLACIER.

▲ 1 ▲

THE ICE TUNNEL INSIDE THE AIGUILLE DU MIDI (12,605 FEET), WHICH EMPTIES AT THE FRENDO SPUR LEADING DOWN TO THE VALLEE BLANCHE. HERE A GROUP OF NUNS HAS COME AS FAR AS TOURISTS CAN GO WITHOUT ROPING UP AND STRAPPING ON CRAMPONS.

musical voice, "Don't worry. Take your time. Everything is fine. You're really doing great." Hah, I say to myself. He's a guide. I know those words. They're not sincere; they're part of the shtick. I've used them myself many times. Nonetheless, I feel better, more secure, as he repeats them, and I find myself standing up, mustering new confidence, and signalling, with thumbs-up, to continue. In another thirty minutes I can smell the breath of the twentieth century: diesel, from the aerial tram. We safely make the final steps up to the ice cave at the Aiguille du Midi, a sharp granite needle 12,605 feet high that is the terminus for the tram. I'm still a bit fuzzy-headed with the altitude, and look up through blurry eyes to see a flock of penguins ready to greet me. I shake my already-spinning head. Am I in the right movie? But as I step closer the birds transform into something almost equally absurd—nuns. They're real, here on holiday.

It is from here we can take the *téléphérique* home. But I can't find my ticket. Nobody rides the cable car down without a ticket. I turn pockets inside out, rip though my pack, but still can't locate that precious piece of cardboard. It's okay, says Serge. He talks to the lift operator, and I'm allowed on board. Serge Obert, the guide de Haute-Montagne for the Compagnie des Guides de Chamonix Mont-Blanc, has done his magic, and his job.

For seven summers I was a river guide on the Colorado River through the Grand Canyon. It was the late sixties and early seventies, and guiding as a career choice was just becoming available. I felt a part of the pioneering generation of guides, who discovered the tricks and tools of the trade as we stumbled through the wilderness pretending to know more than we did—such as how to handle the panicked client. So many times I had to comfort strangers worried about the rapids ahead, or had a client freeze on a narrow ledge, unable to move for fear of falling, as I led a hike up a precipitous side canyon. In my best bedside voice I'd coax the client through, using language much like Serge's. It always worked.

In 1973 I founded SOBEK Expeditions, a company devoted to guiding clients on all sorts of adventures in all manners of landscapes all over the world. Using the guiding techniques I'd helped pioneer on the Colorado, the guides of SOBEK successfully led clients down the Amazon and Zambezi, up Everest and McKinley, and across Patagonia and Borneo.

ONE OF THE PERFECTLY ARTICULATED BARE ROCK PINNACLES THAT DISTINGUISH THE RED NEEDLES NATIONAL PARK.

I felt like a citizen of a fourth world, a free-spirited territory inhabited by neo-Magellans ready to safely escort clients to the ends of the earth for a buck. When a magazine profile credited me as the inventor of adventure travel guiding, I, fatheadedly, believed it. So much so, I asked renowned mountaineer and author David Roberts to write an introduction to our 1984 catalog, asking him to pen a valentine to SOBEK as the originator of adventure travel guiding.

"I can't do that," David protested. "The Compagnie des Guides beat you by a hundred and fifty years."

He was right, of course.

I knew that a Spaniard named Cardenas had beaten me to the Grand Canyon of the Colorado by some four hundred years, but he was no guide in the modern sense. Cardenas' journal exhibits no hint of uplifted sentiments upon this discovery: to him, there was simply this execrable ditch blocking his way. His pragmatic reaction was utterly characteristic of the Renaissance. The notion of wilderness as something other than wasteland was, in the sixteenth century, mostly a luxury yet to be designed. The idea that a voyage

On the trail called Le Grand Balcon Sud, the famous Red Needles frame a view of crenelated peaks and the rounded white summit of Mont Blanc.

through unimproved nature could be good for the psyche would become an invention of the Romantic era, with the first guided trips to the flanks of Mont Blanc. By the 1850s a common sight in the Alps was a string of tourists roped together, the ladies in petticoats and long dresses, disporting upon the glaciers. And the guides on these excursions were from Chamonix, and called their association the Compagnie des Guides.

By HIKING IN THE OFF-SEASON, IT IS POSSIBLE TO WITNESS QUIET SCENES FROM AN EARLIER CENTURY. SOME FORTY THOUSAND PEOPLE TRAVERSE THESE FIELDS AND VALLEYS IN THE BRIEF HIGH SEASON.

As my partners and I struggled to make an international guiding business viable in the 1980s, the competition ballooned. On rivers I pioneered, such as the Bio-Bio in Chile and the Tatshenshini in Alaska, we were once the only guides. Now we had dozens of competitors. In fact, by the beginning of the nineties there were hundreds of guiding companies offering thousands of trips all over the world. SOBEK merged with one, Mountain Travel, the company that founded trekking in Nepal, and still we were practically lost in the classifieds. All of a sudden our guiding company seemed creaky and outgunned. Then I read a news item citing the Compagnie des Guides as not only the oldest guiding organization in the world, but the largest with almost two hundred members. I knew I

THE BOVINE TRAIL IS A SECTION OF THE TOUR DU MONT BLANC, WHICH ACTUALLY FOLLOWS THE ANCIENT CATTLE PATHS ACROSS SEVEN VALLEYS THAT CONNECT THREE COUNTRIES (FRANCE, ITALY, SWITZERLAND), ENCIRCLING THE HIGHEST PEAKS IN WESTERN EUROPE. NOW, TOURISM HAS REPLACED DAIRY FARMING AS THE LEADING ECONOMIC INDUSTRY IN THE REGION.

had to visit this correlative and see if there were messages I was missing.

Now, twenty-five years after guiding my first tour, I was in the company of the Compagnie des Guides, the paterfamilias of the profession. In my years as a guide, and as head of SOBEK, I had run a raft of rivers and organized a number of exotic expeditions, but had never personally climbed a high mountain or participated in a trek. Now I intended to take the classic guided tour, the Tour du Mont Blanc, one of the greatest walks in the world and a mainstay for the Compagnie des Guides. Of the thirty-five thousand people who made the circumnavigation by foot in 1991, seventeen thousand were guided by the Compagnie des Guides. Another four thousand clients were guided to the summit of Mont Blanc itself.

Most trips begin and end in Chamonix, the gorgeous French vale on the north side of the Mont Blanc massif. But, because of scheduling problems, I arranged to join a tour in progress, meeting the group in Issert, Switzerland, for the final days. Then I hoped to continue the circuit with photographer Pamela Roberson, and perhaps conclude the two-week visit with an attempt of Mont Blanc itself, with an able guide from the Compagnie des Guides.

At the Café du Chatelet we meet our group: father-and-son pairs from Portland and Anchorage, and a former SAS flight attendant also living in Alaska. And I meet my confreres, the guides from the Compagnie des Guides, Gilbert Mugnier and Yvan Olianti.

It is quickly evident that no two guides could present a more contrasting study. Yvan, with merry milky blue eyes, is all energy and spunk. With a smile like Magic Johnson, he is a self-confessed clown who tells jokes in any of the four languages (French, Italian, English, and Australian) he professes proficiency. Gilbert, skinny as a snake, exudes a quiet confidence. He rarely volunteers any words, but is always willing to answer questions and ever patient with his guests. Gilbert, who has the long features of a Benedictine monk, comes from mountaineering royalty. His deceased grandfather was one of the most famous Chamonix guides, and his uncle presides as the current president of the Compagnie des Guides.

The routine on this tour changes with the alternating guides and their personalities. While one guide leads the group on the day's hike, the other drives the white Peugeot van carrying everyone's overnight gear. On every hour they communicate by walkie-talkie, and at the end of the day the group arrives at an inn to find all the luggage parked in the rooms and glasses of Grappa ready at the bar. This first afternoon Yvan is our guide, and he regales us with stories as we trek the Swiss Val Ferret. At one point Yvan points out a partially noshed pine cone on the trail, and relates his respect for Gilbert, whom he claims is such a good guide he can tell which hand the squirrel used to eat the pine cone.

THE GREEN NEEDLES OF PINES CONTRAST WITH THE LARCHES, YELLOWING WITH THE FIRST SNAP OF FALL.

At another point we cross above the village of Bourg St. Pierre, and Yvan tells us Napoleon stopped here in the late eighteenth century with forty thousand troops. He put up his men and fed them on credit, and signed a voucher for such. But he never paid. Last year, when François Mitterand stopped by, he was presented the bill. He paid, but refused the interest.

As we make our way this first afternoon I realize how commercial this expedition is. Not only are there TMB (Tour du Mont Blanc) signs with estimated walking times to every landmark at all the intersections, but as we approach the village of Champex there are advertisements posted along the trail for various inns and restaurants, even broadcasting the credit cards accepted.

That night we stay at the Chatlet En Plein Air, an inn with gingham curtains, starchy eiderdowns, and those excess pillows I never quite know how to deploy. Michele Hastler, the owner, says we're the final group for the season, and that after breakfast she's off to the Mediterranean. In fact, with Mont Blanc shrugging off its burden of tourists with the onset of fall, many of the inns have already shut down, making logistics a bit of a challenge for Gilbert and Yvan. Our group doesn't seem to mind. The weather, always an iffy proposition, has been good. And while it can be like EuroDisney in July and August, with thousands packing the paths, we have yet to see another hiker. When not faced with trail ads, I have the evanescent feeling we are truly alone in the wilderness.

Over a fondue dinner, Yvan takes off in wide narrative gyres. He reveals that before joining the Compagnie des Guides he had worked in an adult bookstore in Australia, which somehow gave him the necessary experience to handle people in awkward situations. He tells of the time in the winter of 1982 he was hired to coordinate a scheme to drive a red Peugeot 104 down the east face of Mont Blanc. The car was helicoptered to the top, yet only negotiated four hundred yards before darkness. The following day the police arrested the driver, and the stunt was never completed. Yvan speaks in antic, broad, big-breathed sentences. Even when he goes over the morrow's itinerary his words flow in a slangy, belt-of-kirsch surge, intimate and muscular. Yvan drives with two wheels over the edge and no regrets in his rearview mirror.

Before heading out Monday morning, we pack our individual lunches from a table of goodies that includes fresh fruit, flaky croissants, yogurt, gorp, Appenzell and Gruyere cheese, thick-crusted bread, and pepperoni. We're in "Sweetzerland," the land of chocolate, so I expect an array of the country's finest, but instead the basket is filled with Snickers and Mars bars.

The day finds us hoofing it over the Bovine Trail. Fittingly, the trail is drenched with the gamelan-like sounds of cowbells. It winds through a checkerboard of forest and field, up through *Heidi*-esque farms closed for the winter. It also twines by sprigs of sweet, ripe blueberries, and at every chance we go grazing. The scenery eludes us, however. The clouds have drifted in and boxed the silky air.

The next day we scramble up a trail that gropes like an enormous sentence, run-

ning across the Col de Balme (7,188 feet), the Smuggler's Route into France. We stop for lunch at the pass, the border, and sip sweet red wine schlepped to the top by Yvan. And we watch the glossy black choughs, the birds French poets summon as symbols of death, watching us and waiting for our crumbs.

Pine forests along the Smuggler's Route from Switzerland into France.

As we descend, it begins to drizzle, jacketing the rocks with a satiny sheen. Believing somehow that Gore-Tex represents international inoculation against bad weather, I struggle to pull my North Face gear from my pack. Yvan, with the indifference of a mountain ungulate, simply unfurls a green and white Wilson golf umbrella and merrily bounces along.

That evening we're stationed in the village of le Buet, in the only inn that's still open, where we're met in the lobby by a gracious, furry, five-month-old cat, Mimine. Our fluffy host purrs a welcome, and then follows me to my room to make sure everything meets my satisfaction. As it turns out, the Hotel du Buet is just a short drive from Gilbert's two-hundred-year-old family farm, la Boerne, and Gilbert invites us for dinner. For generations the Mugnier farm managed by raising dairy cattle, but the short alpine summer, rough terrain, and increased competition from the lowlands have undermined the traditional livelihood. Now only Gilbert's brother, Pierre, continues the family legacy, trying to eke out a living raising cattle on the mountainside. Gilbert has spent his free time the last few years converting a major section of the farmhouse into an auberge. He now has forty dormitory-style beds, a sauna, and hundreds of Mont Blanc trekkers a year stopping in for the evening and a meal.

The yellow squash soup is savory, the wood-grilled saibling sweet, and after a few pousse-cafés our faces gleam with alpineglow. We start to swap guiding tales of ill-prepared clients. I tell of a harried attorney who appeared for a Grand Canyon raft tour with a white suit, dancing shoes, and a case of cold duck, thinking his secretary had booked him on a river *cruise,* complete with big band. Yvan tops me with the story of a woman who showed up keen to begin her photographic career shooting the Alps. She was delighted when she heard the only thing she would have to carry would be her camera, as all other gear would be bused around. But Yvan couldn't help but notice how she strained under the weight of her bulky day pack the first morning. It wasn't until the first view of Mont Blanc that the mystery was solved. As everyone pulled out cameras, the woman with the heavy pack hauled out a Kodak slide projector and innocently asked Yvan how the camera worked. Worse yet, she only had print film.

THE AUTHOR ON THE FAR SIDE OF THE COL DE BONHOMME, WHERE THE TRAIL SPILLS TOWARD ITALY, A SIDE OF MONT BLANC THAT IS MORE ARCHITECTURALLY SUBLIME.

Gilbert wakes us at the first peep of dawn, announcing this to be the toughest day of the tour: an ascent of Mont Buet, or Lady's Mont Blanc, nicknamed for the nineteenth-century wives who would climb the 10,164-foot summit to watch their mountaineering husbands clamber up the real thing across the dale. Because Buet Village, our starting point, is a bit more than 4,000 feet above sea level, this means a round-trip altitude gain and loss of 12,000 feet in one day—no stroll to the corner video store.

The first few hours we trail along a calcareous, gray stream, l'Eau de Bérard, and through matted pastures filled with cows. The larches are yellowing, and the sky is puffed with clouds. About noon we cross a gauntlet of chalky scree and reach the snow line. I'm last in line, and have fallen well behind the group. I keep telling myself it's because I stop and take photos, but I'm feeling out of shape and still a bit jet-lagged from the long flight. But then as I step slowly upwards I notice peculiar tracks in the snow. I look closer and see they are paw tracks, weaving in and out of the

A GALAXY OF GLACIERS CARVES AND SHAPES THE UNIVERSE OF THE FRENCH ALPS. THE AVERAGE FLOW SPEED OF THE GLACIERS HERE IS 260 FEET PER YEAR. THE SPEED REACHES 3,000 FEET PER YEAR AT THE POINT OF FALL; THE MOVEMENT IS MORE RAPID AT THE CENTER THAN AT THE EDGES.

footprints left by Gilbert and the clients. What animal could be at this altitude? A snow leopard? Why would it follow in the oblique footsteps of our group? The mystery keeps my mind occupied as I climb, and then at last I see Gilbert and the gang waiting on an outcropping just ahead.

In a few more steps I catch up, at La Table au Chantre, a saddle at almost 9,000 feet, and Gilbert's designated lunch spot. My first question is about the cat tracks, and suddenly Mimine, the host cat from Hotel du Buet, bounds over and begins to rub against my leg while purring. Everyone on our aerie flashes a Cheshire grin. Gilbert explains that Mimine followed the group up the mountain, and every time someone tried to turn her back, she refused, and merrily padded alongside the Vibram souls.

It is still another hour to the summit, and so after a repast of cheese and brown bread, Gilbert starts scampering upwards like a squirrel. Mimine bounces along behind. "Stop!" yells Pamela, "You can't let the cat continue. It's too high and too cold." So Pamela grabs the wayward cat, and announces she'll head back down and chaperon Mimine. As Pamela is left behind petting Mimine, off go the rest of us for the final pitch.

I feel about as heavy and laggard as one of Hannibal's elephants as we trudge up the mountain. I can see some chamois grazing a thousand feet below, and can't help but think they, creatures of these landscapes, know the right place to be, and it isn't here. As we step higher, my lightweight Supplex Taffeta jacket feels like wet wool, I'm sweating like Nixon, and my camera feels like a slide projector. Gilbert, however, who walks through the wet snow like a whisper, is singing, and I find myself drawn to his voice, and the back of his shaggy head. Then, in a trice, we're at the top. It feels like we're standing on four million scoops of vanilla ice cream. Across the way Mont Blanc becomes almost impudently visible, the first time she has shown her face to me. She seems to be smiling between the unwinding clouds, and I smile back. Then, as quickly as they parted, the clouds slam shut across the sky, like the door of an observatory dome.

On our descent, we look back upwards during a water break and see the silhouette of an alpine ibex, his croissantlike horns pointing in the direction of the Aiguilles Rouges range. While news of ecological ruination is commonly heard throughout the Alps, this ruminant points to quite a different story. About 150 years ago, over-hunting reduced the European ibex population to about fifty. It looked as though the closest an alpinist might ever get to an ibex would be the constellation Capricorn. But tough protective laws and reintroduction of captive-bred ibex into the mountains have brought the numbers up to an estimated twenty-two thousand, one of the most successful conservation projects ever.

In the final hour of our descent it seems oddly quiet. And then—cowabunga!—I realize there are no clanging cowbells. In the time it took for us to hike up and back to this spot, the herd was moved off the mountain for the season. As we descend a bit farther we see a figure hunched over the path staring into a field of bluebells. Once we're a little closer, we see it's Pamela, practically in tears. "I lost the cat," she says with big eyes. Apparently soon after we left for the summit, Mimine bolted down a cliff toward some mountain goats, and Pamela couldn't follow. She yelled for an hour, and finally gave up and headed down. The loss, and the thought of Mimine trying to survive the night at 9,000 feet, hung over her for the rest of the walk. "Don't worry," Gilbert says in his most tranquilizing guide voice. "You made a fox or an eagle very happy." Pamela simpers.

Back at the Hotel du Buet we tell Mimine's owner, Veronique Chamel, about the disappearance. She just shrugs and says Mimine had climbed halfway up the mountain a half dozen times, but always returned. She isn't worried.

Thursday is the final day of the commercial tour, and it takes us up into Red Needles National Park, where Gilbert was once a ranger. This is the most spectacular day yet, as we wan-

THE ENDLESS SWEEP OF THE VALLEE BLANCHE ("WHITE VALLEY"), A SECRET WORLD, FROZEN INTO AN ALMOST OTHER-WORLDLY LACK OF MOTION.

THE AUTHOR ASCENDING A PASS ON THE MONT BLANC CIRCUIT. THE TREK IS ONE OF SEEMINGLY END- LESS ASCENTS AND DESCENTS, AVERAGING 9,000 FEET IN ELEVA- TION CHANGE A DAY.

der between great, rough-hewn crenellations of bare rock thrusting up into the delft blue sky. All the peaks seem to be perfectly articulated, especially Mont Blanc, whose royal ranking is marked by a flossy nimbus crown. We follow the arc of the sun across le Grand Balcon Sud for much of the after- noon, and gape across the valley at a sea of glaciers and a fleet of peaks looking like the prows of racing sloops. Occasionally the luminous stillness is inter- rupted by the crack and echo of a distant explosion, and we wonder if it is a glacier calving. Or a crystal hunter. (Gilbert told us two members of the Compagnie des Guides had recently been arrested for illegally dynamiting glaciers during crystal hunts.) Instead, we later learn, it's controlled dynamiting, blasting out water pockets in the glaciers before they become too large and burst on their own and flood the valley. In the seventeenth century, icebergs from these glacier bursts would float all the way into Geneva. Back then priests would trek to the glaciers and exorcise them with biblical words; now they reach the hot spots by Alouette II helicopters, and exorcise them with TNT.

We know we're getting close to Chamonix when we begin to see other people: a man with a shotgun and his dog off to hunt black grouse and pheasant; a couple of mountain bikers pumping by in fluorescent Lycra; and parasailers above. We're dropping into the sports *creperie* of the world.

We're parked at the Hotel Croix Blanche in downtown Chamonix, nestled between the world's most expensive Patagonia outlet and a Century 21 office hawking million-dollar properties. This fairytale town's true religion is mountaineering, and the temple is just a block away, Maison de la Montagne, headquarters of the Compagnie des Guides.

After a group dinner at Bar Nash, the legendary postwar haunt of British mountaineers, we sip pear brandy and talk about the immediate future. Yvan is heading off to Tuscany to guide another trip and our fellow hikers are returning to the U.S. Pamela and I intend to stick around for another week exploring the neighborhood, and Gilbert offers to be our guide.

Gilbert drives us to Les Houches at the lower end of the Chamonix Valley for a hike over the ridge to Les Contamines. The weather report does not look good he tells us, and storms are predicted for the next several days. When he drops us off he leaves me with a walkie-talkie and says he'll be listening in case we have problems. Immediately the clouds flood in, and we ramble alongside the lonesome metal pylons of a closed ski lift. On the far side of the Col de Voza it begins to pour, and we gamely march between the spruce and pine in near zero vis-

FROM THE HEIGHTS OF FRANCE'S AIGUILLE DU MIDI, LOOKING ACROSS THE STORMFRONT TO THE ITALIAN ALPS.

ibility. Finally I'm so thoroughly soaked and chilled I feel like a crustacean with its shell off, and I call Gilbert on the radio. In minutes his van crawls up the road hauling deliverance.

As we bump into Les Contamines, Gilbert points out Mont Joie on the right, peeking through a tear in the clouds. On the other side I notice a hotel called Mount Joy, the English translation of the overhanging peak. For some reason it reminds me of Joy Carber, née Joy Ungricht, the first female international river guide. She shared many guiding trips with me, including rafting explorations down the Indus and Zambezi rivers. Once, in Pakistan, we were caught in an enormous rapid, just the two of us in a fifteen-foot inflatable with a broken oar. Somehow, working together, we managed to wrestle through. Afterwards we hugged and giddily admitted we both felt invulnerable, immortal. That was thirteen years ago. Three years ago Joy married another SOBEK guide, Butch Carber, in a ceremony on top of Mount Kilimanjaro. Less than three weeks later, at a Utah clinic for a routine parasite check, she was diagnosed with colon cancer. The doctors gave her weeks to live. When I took her to the movies last Christmas (to see

Aᴛ ᴛʜᴇ sʜᴏᴜʟᴅᴇʀ ᴏf Mᴏɴᴛ Bʟᴀɴᴄ, ʟᴏᴏᴋɪɴɢ ᴀᴄʀᴏss ᴛᴏ ᴛʜᴇ Cʜᴀɪɴᴇ ᴅᴇs Aʀᴀᴠɪs.

Hook), her elfin face was drawn and exhausted; she had lost thirty pounds of muscle from her tiny frame, and was in great pain. But she laughed and loved the movie about a grown-up Peter Pan who once again chooses love over immortality.

I ask Gilbert if there are any women in the Compagnie des Guides, and he replies, yes, one: Sylviane Tavernier, a champion downhill skier and accomplished mountain climber. Although the first woman, Marie Paradis, stood on the summit of Mont Blanc back in 1808, it was 1985 before the phallocentric group allowed a woman to be a member guide. Gilbert shows me a photograph of Sylviane, who is leading a trek in Nepal at the moment. She has the same slight physique and free smile as Joy.

WHEN THE DARKNESS AND LAYERS OF FOG SHEATH THE VALLEYS, THE MASSIF OF MONT BLANC RISES INTO THE LIGHT.

That night we are the only ones in our hotel, and it seems dank and lonely. I play pool with the cook, and listen to French rap music on the jukebox. When I return to the room I receive a phone call from my office in California. The news is sad. Joy Ungricht Carber died last Tuesday. "One trip has to end so another can begin," Joy remarked while on the Colorado just weeks before. Outside the window, a bluish star hangs over the mountain like a tear.

Mount Joie is wrapped in fresh snow the next morning. Gilbert drives us to and drops us off at the Notre Dame de la Gorge, the start of a two-thousand-year-old Roman path that coils into Italy. If not for the trash cans and benches every couple hundred yards, this could be the Appian Way. At an esplanade called La Balme, we witness a study in generations. An ancient Willy's jeep rumbles up, and out hops an old

Chamoniard in a Tirolean hat with a shepherd's crook of laburnum wood and a worn leather backpack. At his side is a bow-legged mutt. But as he takes off hiking, the new generation passes him by. Along comes a young man sprayed in Spandex sprinting up the hill, poling with his aluminum Leki poles, his German Shepherd at his side. Neither acknowledges the other as each reaches into the mountains for his own special joy.

Absorbed in memories of Joy, I make the final pitch up to the Col de Bonhomme (7,641 feet). Though Pamela is hiking with me, I feel entirely alone and am focused on my thoughts. The present steals me back when I step onto the shoulder and a rude and different air slaps my face. A small hut straddles the crest, and I rush inside and slam shut the door. The little planked room looks like a bus-station bathroom. Not only is it littered with the tourist spore of tinfoil, cans, bottles, and empty propane canisters, but almost every inch of wall space is scrawled with graffiti. Never before have I faced obscenities in a dozen languages. It is, I think, becoming increasingly difficult to experience the ultimate payoff of wilderness travel—a peaceful moment of lonely exhilaration on a silent mountain ridge. How could alpinists be so willing to soil the precarious beauty they work so hard to visit? The hut, providing shelter on its postcard perch from a brutal wind, reflects the best and worst of our culture. Thankfully I notice that signatures from Yvan and Gilbert are nowhere to be seen on these walls. So I sit back to eat lunch and read the invading wit and wisdom of hikers from around the world.

The afternoon spills toward Italy, a side of Mont Blanc that seems more architecturally solemn. Gilbert picks us up in a sheep pasture just above the hamlet of Les Chapieux. Because all the inns in Italy are closed for the season, he takes us to the nearest hotel, the Hotel L'Autantic in Bourg Saint-Maurice, one of the Olympic sites. Tomorrow, Gilbert promises, we'll tackle the Italian side of the Tour du Mont Blanc, and in a couple days we'll connect the dots and meet our starting point at Issert in Switzerland.

But it is not to be. The morning is a mess, thick as French espresso. It's just not worth the effort, so we ask Gilbert to take us back to Chamonix through the gaping hole bored through Mont Blanc's innards, the 7.2-mile-long tunnel. The Alps, once an almost insurmountable barrier between north and south, are now crossed by more than fifty airlines, seven rail services, thirty major highways, and a tunnel through the belly of Mont Blanc. The most violent avalanches long ago overcame the laws of gravity, rolling from the lowlands upwards. They consist of thousands of cars carrying thousands of people looking for mountain solitude. Last year, 800,000 trucks and 4 million passenger cars passed through this tunnel, and developers now want to bore a second shaft. And the results of all this visiting fossil fuel have not been scenic. Acid rain and smog have killed great swaths of vital forest, contributing to avalanches and mud slides. Half of the Alps' native animal and bird species have disappeared. The solution? According to Gilbert, it would be to banish all motorized traffic in the Alps, and welcome only those who wish to walk. And he would happily be their guide.

Once through the tunnel, the weather is still tenebrous. In the inimitable guide way, Gilbert tries to comfort us. He says he's guided summer trips during which it rained every day, and he had to show the clients postcards of the scenery they missed.

AUTUMNAL DUSK BATHES THE VALLEY OF CHAMONIX, AS SEEN FROM THE FLANKS OF MONT BLANC.

As it turns out the next four days are equally gloomy, not worth the effort of a major hike. I use the time to explore Chamonix, visit the famous Musée Alpin, browse the boutiques, take a brief hike above town along le Grand Balcon Nord (and even here the valley is filmed in purple clouds, so thick I can't even see the high steeple of the eighteenth-century priory), and visit the famous Compagnie des Guides. Gilbert spends much of his day under the copper roof of the Maison de la Montagne, as he is the organization's treasurer, and it is here I meet M. Jean-Claude Charlet, Gilbert's uncle and the current president of the Compagnie des Guides. Jean-Claude volunteers the company's history.

The original guides in the region were mostly crystal hunters, recruited to escort curious foreigners into the high mountains. But as the number of visitors to the Alps increased in the early nineteenth century, it became essential to eliminate the numerous cadgers who accosted strangers on the roads, offering services for which they were not suitably qualified. In 1820, Mont Blanc had its first critical climbing accident when three unskilled guides were blown into a crevasse and died. The following year, Compagnie des Guides of Chamonix was officially founded with thirty-four licensed guides, and received its first statutes in 1823 from the King of Sardinia. Admission to the Compagnie des Guides was exclusive, requiring a long internship, passing scores on a tough exam, and that candidates be natives of Chamonix. This policy continued until 1930, when the first outsider was admitted. Today about a third hail from beyond the twelve-mile-long valley, though all still must be French born.

Guiding is a risky profession, with an average accidental on-duty death for every other year of the company's existence. But for every guide lost, many mountain patrons have been saved. For years the guides were known as the Saint Bernards of the summits, as they conducted all the mountain rescues. But in 1969 the government established a high-mountain police platoon to handle the rescues, leaving the Compagnie des Guides as a nonprofit commercial guiding group.

Today the organization finds itself faced with steep competition, and the loss of some of its best members to more profitable pursuits, such as crystal hunting, which has enjoyed a New Age resurgence. So the organization is retooling itself for survival into the twenty-first century. It is producing its own line of clothing; it plans to offer guiding tours beyond the Alps, to Nepal, Africa, Alaska, and even Mexico; it intends to produce slick color brochures in English; and it is considering the once unthinkable: allowing guides from other countries. However, Jean-Claude Charlet, who has been a member of the Compagnie des Guides for fifteen years, believes the future is ultimately linked to the spirituality of guiding, to the preservation of an ethos and a place where two people, one expert, the other novice, can join hands and rediscover themselves.

As the rain sluices down I tell Gilbert I'd like to make a try at the high-fiber stuff, Mont Blanc itself, and ask if he'll guide me. He says no, for a couple of reasons. He is strictly a hiking guide, one of about two dozen in the Compagnie des Guides, and doesn't want to guide at altitude. Too risky. He has seen too many deaths, including that of another uncle, Jean-Paul Charlet, who died in an avalanche eight years before on the slopes of la Vormaine, a glacier not far from the family farm. The other reason is the storms have dropped too much snow and the trail, which is packed by the feet of up to three hundred climbers a day in the summer, is covered and thus too difficult and dangerous for a tenderfoot like me. However, he says there is an alternative (a good guide always has an alternative). If the weather breaks he will arrange for an alpine guide to take us on the gondola up to Aiguille du Midi, across the edge of the Vallée Blanche to one of the highest hotels in the world, the Refuge des Cosmiques, just a little over a year old, and leased long-term by the Compagnie des Guides. From there I could attempt a crossing of the Vallée Blanche and the Glacier du Geant, over the roof of Europe, all the way to Italy.

It seems the ideal conclusion to my survey, and I pray for clear skies as the week

wears on. But every morning I awake to a hood of gray. It seems there is a kind of anti-sun here, pouring out lead, not light. Then on Thursday the sun warms my wool blanket, and awakens me to watch, with hungry eyes, as it brushes away the mists. Mont Blanc's gentle dome glows against a hard, blue sky.

Gilbert introduces me to my guide for the attempt, Serge Obert, 32, a clear-eyed, five-year member of the Compagnie des Guides. He schedules an afternoon ascent on the tram, and so with a few hours to spare Pamela asks Gilbert to drive us to the Hotel du Buet to ask about Mimine the cat. When we arrive the place is shuttered, no life apparent. I knock at the various doors and windows, and then out back Veronique, Mimine's owner, appears. She reports that Mimine never returned, but that was fine. Mimine was always an independent sort, magnetically drawn to the mountains, and is probably content with her

THE CHAMONIX VALLEY ENTERED THE REALM OF HISTORY IN 1091, WHEN THE COUNT OF GENEVA AND HIS SON GAVE IT TO THE BENEDICTINE MONKS OF SAINT MICHEL DE LA CLUSE, WHO IN TURN BUILT A PRIORY HERE. IN THE EIGHTEENTH CENTURY, THE VALLEY BECAME THE CRADLE OF ALPINE TOURISM AFTER TWO ENGLISH EXPLORERS PUBLISHED AN ACCOUNT OF THEIR JOURNEYS THROUGH THE HIGH LANDSCAPES ABOVE THE SCENIC VALLEY.

place. It was consistent with the philosophy of mountaineers the world over, and of the guides I knew: specifically, that everyone has a right to climb and to encounter danger on his or her own terms. It is the danger, the toll, of living free.

Sometime midafternoon the gondola door slides back at the Aiguille du Midi, and it feels as if I'm standing in front of a freezer. We clomp over a catwalk and through a tunnel, and at the crisp edge of the snow, Serge shows me how to put on the crampons, rope up, and use the ice ax. This is all new to me, and as I bend over to fasten my crampon, I feel the woozy effects of altitude. I'm a bit spooked by the prospects ahead. But before I have time to rethink the exercise, Serge has me stepping down the steep, much-exposed Frendo spur to the vertical realm of the Vallée Blanche. It seems like a secret world, frozen into an almost supernatural lack of motion. We trudge through the deep snow for perhaps ninety minutes before making a brief ascent to the Refuge des Cosmiques, a radiant harbor in the middle of a wide ocean of white. Only two others share the 130-bed refuge with us, climbers from Barcelona hoping to make the same traverse to Italy in the morning. They, too, were waiting for the sunshine for days, and we all feel a proprietary attachment now that it has arrived.

The Refuge des Cosmiques is managed by Thevenet Marie-Nöelle, a sweet-faced, middle-aged woman with hair that might have been cut with a Swiss Army knife. She greets us with a wide grin and big bowls of Schlag-topped hot chocolate in a common room decorated with fresh flowers. For dinner she whips up a four-course meal, featuring crisp vegetables and boeuf bourguignonne (what else but haute cuisine here?). The sunset is a symphony of light from this belvedere, spilling exquisite fluidlike color across the Chaîne des Aravis. The harvest moon, whiter than the brightest glacier, rises like a ball of rolling mercury into the clear blue-gray eastern sky, then trips along the crests of the Italian Alps, growing rounder and fuller every second.

All the bunk rooms are named after famous guides, and we're assigned to the Armand Charlet, Gilbert's grandfather, which seems auspicious. Serge suggests over dinner that we drink a bit of red wine to combat the effects of altitude, which often make it difficult to sleep. Nevertheless, despite quaffing an entire bottle of Domaine Sainte-Anne (1990), I have a headache and can't force unconsciousness.

Morning comes all too quickly, and with it disappointment. The weather, so friendly the day before, has turned on us. It is dark, windy, and snowing. With only off-piste terrain, there is risk of falling into a crevasse. The Spaniards announce they are giving up and heading back. Still, Serge, in the traditional optimistic mood of guides, urges a try, so we suit up and head out.

But an hour into the hike it is apparent the weather is getting worse, and breaking trail in the new snow is like wading through a knee-deep gumbo. Serge evaluates the weather conditions and my condition, and makes the difficult decision to head back to the Aiguille du Midi. And it is the right decision. Today I don't have The White Stuff.

The following afternoon I'm having a last beer with Gilbert in the Hôtel du Rhône in Geneva before catching the Swiss Air flight back to Los Angeles. I finally muster the courage to ask a question that plagued me for my years as a guide, and that troubles every guide I know: "What are you going to do when you get old?"

A sly smile curls over Gilbert's thirty-eight-year-old rucksack face. "I'm going to keep on guiding forever," he declares. "I think I have one of the luckiest jobs in the world. I can't believe I get paid to walk through the mountains. I love walking, and will always love it, and as long as I can walk, I will guide..."

There was some kind of satori in these words. It's not the company that continues; it is the guiding, the sharing of a passion for places beautiful and wild, the combined effort to open the gates to our dreams, to explore inexhaustible kingdoms. Guiding will be around long after any business I'm a part of, and well after the guides I've known have left to explore the last bend in the river or the other side of the white mountain.

Always get a second opinion.

— Dr. George Fuller, tropical medicine
expert, upon diagnosing his own schistosomiasis
after a river trip in East Africa, 1973

SNOW WAY OUT:
KILIMANJARO

The wake-up call is just after midnight. Daniel, our guide, is standing over me with a cup of steaming hot tea and a yellow smile. Rolling out of the bunk, I clutch at my toilet bag. Dr. Nelson repeatedly ordered me to take my daily dosage of Zestril, a 10-mg tablet for high blood pressure. I've been remiss in keeping to the regimen, but here, on the mountain, he said it was critical. And this is summit day, the day I had been anticipating for weeks.

I open the toilet bag, and pull out the bottle of Zestril. But the cap is off, the bottle empty. I grope in the bag and retrieve another bottle, and see the label for codeine. It too is empty, the top off. And in the bottom of my bag, there's a pile of pills, all indistinguishable in the half-light of the hut. I need to take the Zestril to get up the mountain, so I pick a pill and pop it in. It will either propel me upward with dilated arteries, or put me to sleep.

Up to this point the highest I had ever been, outside of a plane, was 14,495 feet at the summit of Mount Whitney, the tallest mountain in the continental United States. Although I had made the ascent fifteen years earlier, I remember clearly it was a tough effort for me. I had a headache, felt nauseated, and struggled with every

THE SNOWS OF KILIMANJARO. KILIMANJARO'S GLACIAL DOME, SOARING ABOVE THE PLAINS, IS INSTANTLY RECOGNIZED WORLDWIDE AS AFRICA'S HIGHEST MOUNTAIN.

G AZING TOWARD KILIMANJARO, THE SOURCE OF ALL LIFE IN THE AREA.

step. I had an epiphany at the top. I realized mountain climbing was not for me. This would be my ceiling.

Yet here I was, off into the high chill with five layers of clothing, heading up the final pitch of the highest mountain in Africa—Kilimanjaro, at 19,340 glaciated feet above the sea.

I think about my toe. The big toe on my left foot. As we plod ever higher in the icy, burning blackness, I wiggle my toe, sheathed in three layers of socks and my guaranteed waterproof boots. It moves, feels fine, except for a tingle inspired by Diamox, the diuretic that helps prevent altitude sickness by draining fluid from the lungs. Nobody says a word. Though we began as a dozen first-timers, we have splintered into smaller groups. Pamela, stricken by altitude sickness, was retching last night. With the aid of four Tanzanian guides she had stumbled off toward the Horombo complex of huts, back at 12,336 feet, to recover. Mike has bloody sputum; Rhea has diarrhea; Patrick is constipated; Carl and Susan are attorneys; Dana, a forty-one-year-old California river guide who has come to work the mountain, is wondering if he's too old for this profession. We are all trespassing here. Yet, five of us march out in a knot: Dr. Steve, Bob, Lee, Gary, and me. The headlamps atop our hunched figures cut into the raw, inky air as we follow the trail's zigs and zags up this vertical gravel pit. It feels good to walk.

Now in my mind I hear the words: *"There is the possibility you may never walk again." Eight months ago, March 24, I was in Hawaii, re-cooping after an exhausting cross-country lecture tour. I was renegade diving in Maui. Renegade because I was never certified as a Scuba diver, had never completed a*

course, though I'd tooled around with a tank and regulator in Bali, the Caribbean, and the Tuamotus without ill effects. Yet this time something seemed different. I didn't feel quite right as I swam among the coral-colored fish in Ahihi Bay, and was oddly pleased when the fifty-minute dive was over.

The next morning at 3:00 A.M. we left our hotel to drive to the top of Haleakala, the two-mile-high volcano that looms over Maui. We arrived in time for sunrise, then saddled up on bikes for a six-hour ride down what had to

THE WEATHER SPAWNED BY KILIMANJARO HAS SIRED A SERIES OF SHALLOW LAKES, WHICH FEED THE AVIFAUNA—INCLUDING MASSES OF PINK FLAMIN-GOS—OF EAST AFRICA.

be the steepest paved road on earth. But halfway down a sharp pain bayoneted my left leg. It spread as we continued, and became nearly unbearable by evening. I visited the airport nurse the next morning before boarding a flight home, and she recommended I drink as much alcohol as possible while flying, since she couldn't prescribe any painkillers.

I think about that pain as we continue the climb. The air is thin and dry. It doesn't crowd, it doesn't weigh. We are moving like astronauts, in slow motion, bodies bent into the mountain.

Kilimanjaro is only two degrees south of the equator, but as we ascend its flanks we pass through five climatic zones roughly parallel to the vegetation belts one might encounter travelling from the equator north or south toward the poles. And we seem to be tracing nature's evolution in reverse, from the big animals at the base to the first stirrings of bacterial life on the high reaches of this ancient cone. I like this skein of change that unwinds before me with every footfall.

A Masai woman looks to the past and future, which are much the same for her. Whereas most Africans have shed traditional customs and dress, the Masai have kept their cultural heritage intact, remained visibly connected to their identity and indifferent to the alleged benefits of modern society.

Once back in Oakland I saw my doctor, who guessed my muscles had locked up and sent me home to a heating pad and bed. Yet even with a pharmacy of pills—Flexeril, Vicodin, and Naprosyn—the pain sharpened, and spread to my other leg. Then my left toes turned cold and began to go numb. This could mean nerve damage, so Pamela rushed me to the emergency room. I had a spinal tap, a CT scan, and two MRIs. The diagnosis: I had something called a spinal-dural arteriovenous fistula, or a hole between an artery and a vein. The blood was shunting the wrong way, creating ischemic pressure against my spine, and I could become paralyzed.

After two and a half hours switchbacking through the obsidian night, we clamber into Meyer's Cave at 17,000 feet. Only 2,340 feet to go, I calculate with much difficulty. It seems unsporting that a shallow cave is all that is named after Dr. Hans Meyer, the German geologist who first breathed the rarefied atmosphere of Kilimanjaro's white roof in 1889. Yet it is a cave of mythic architecture. For a long time the Chagga people who lived at the underpinnings of Kilimanjaro refused to pass beyond this grotto, believing it was the entrance to the "House of the Dead." Now Daniel spits into the cave, which he says is for good luck.

I take a maintenance break and choke down some water. The primary thief at altitude is dehydration, yet at the same time it's tough to carry much water. I have three quarts, which is about half of what's recommended for a day at altitude. I also note my internal sphygmomanometer. I'm groggy, but not sleepy, so I must have swallowed the right pill. My luck hadn't been as good a couple days earlier. We were taking an acclimation day at Horombo Hut, wandering among the giant heather, pulling on the mosslike lichen known as old man's beard. I began taking Diamox, the drug of choice on this contour line. On the second evening I was feeling quite chipper, and told Carl, one of my roommates in the hut, that the Diamox was truly a miracle drug and that it was working wonderfully, except perhaps for a touch of diarrhea. The following morning I went to take another dosage, and looked closely at the bottle. I hadn't been taking Diamox, but rather Bactrim, which supposedly curbs dysentery.

Appetite is nonexistent at this level, but I force down a boiled sweet and a bite of a wild berry PowerBar. Then off again on the predawn slog.

THE SNOWY SUMMIT OF KIBO LOOMS OVER THE ALPINE DESERT OF THE SADDLE, THE WINDSWEPT SHOULDER CONNECTING THE FRATERNAL PEAKS OF THE GREAT WHITE MOUNTAIN.

Just before putting me under, the anesthesiologist held a clipboard in front of me with a release I had to sign. He explained there was a chance I might not wake up, that I could die. I didn't have time to think about silence as an ecumenical state before the nitrous oxide swam through the mask and the sodium pentothal penetrated my blood. Counting backwards I made it to ninety-seven before oblivion.

It's getting harder to concentrate as we crunch up the cinder cone, the lava scree shifting like shards of glass. The slope angles about fifty-five degrees, and the loose gravel swallows a good portion of every step. I need assistance, and so turn on my Walkman. Earlier in the trip I tried a series of tapes as we trudged the seven and one-half spongy miles through dark moorland between the Mandara and Horombo huts. I sampled the Brandenburg Concertos, Sade, Bonnie Raitt, Marvin Gaye, Ladysmith Black Mambazo, Michael Bolton, James Taylor, and Cream. Nothing seemed to have the right energy to move my feet along. This time I punch in Aretha Franklin, and when she begins to wail "Natural Woman," I can't control my face. Euphoria tears across. I feel great, and my body moves to some ancestral beat.

THE MASAI ARE AS MUCH A PART OF THE LANDSCAPE AS THE THORN TREES. EACH MAN MAY HAVE AS MANY WIVES AS HE CAN SUPPORT, BUT EACH WIFE MUST HAVE HER OWN HUT.

After two rounds of Aretha it's time to change tunes. We stop for a water break, and I go through the complex task of changing tapes. It

seems like calculus. Finally, I slip in Bobby Brown and find myself jack swinging with new vigor. My head seems unclouded, my anatomic checklist shows no red lights. I even have CCU (clear, copious urine), a good sign. Just the night before, as we tucked in after watery soup and a game of Hearts, my head was pounding, my stomach protesting, and I felt I might vomit. I took a Diamox, two aspirin, and a Halcion. Better climbing through chemistry. Dr. Steve, a gastroenterologist and our oldest member at fifty-four, is the most vocally obsessed with making it to the top, and has been taking dexamethasone (a steroid) prophylactically. His demon is altitude; he gets headaches when he flies into Denver. (Incidentally, doctors have the lowest summiting rate of any profession because they're often unwilling to

A BLACK RHINO GREETING. THE FEMALE IS OFTEN ACCOMPANIED BY SUBADULTS OR ITS CALF. TICK BIRDS, OFTEN CALLED OXPECKERS, USUALLY ESCORT RHINOS AND ACT AS SECURITY ALARMS. IN THE DAYS WHEN ERNEST HEMINGWAY HUNTED HERE, RHINOS WERE THE FAVORED TROPHY. TODAY RHINOS ARE KILLED FOR THEIR HORNS, WHICH ARE SOLD FOR OBSCENE PRICES AND USED AS DAGGER HANDLES BY THE YEMENIS AND APHRODISIACS BY THE CHINESE. POACHING HAS ALMOST DRIVEN THE ARMOR-PLATED ANIMALS INTO OBLIVION.

Thorn trees are common on the lower flanks of Kilimanjaro. Their flat-topped shape has become as emblematic of Africa as the great mountain itself. They are legumes and their highly nutritious beanlike seedpods are popular with elephants, antelopes, rhinos, and baboons.

The Simba River hippo pool, on the Tanzanian side of Kilimanjaro. The "river horses," as the ancient Greeks called them, weigh up to six thousand pounds each and spend their days lolling in water and nights foraging along the banks, shovelling down some two hundred pounds of grass per meal.

take the advice of the guides, and are always taking medicine for everything.) We all have demons
here. Bob, the ex-marine, suffers from bad knees
and Bill Clinton's promise to admit gays into the
military. Lee agonizes privately about his weight.
Gary, who has the cautious temperament of a
chemist, which he is, is in a bad marriage. I roll
around my sleeping bag considering if I'm going
to become sick, wondering if I'll have the stuff to
reach the summit. I have an excuse, I tell myself. I
can always go down on the pretense I want to
assist Pamela. But I feel like a spy in my own
soul. I can't fool myself.

Two miles high we push into the moorlands, which are filled with exotic plants and shrubs, including lobelias, proteas, and various daisylike flowers. The cone in the distance is a sacred site where locals send their holy men to pray for rain.

The sky is beginning to lighten, and as
the silhouette of a wall appears above me I turn off my headlamp. For a moment the
mountain looks like it's receding, and I stop to calibrate myself. I've been third in our
alpine chain gang, but Lee passes me at this point. *"Pole, pole,"* is the Swahili mantra I
breathe to myself. It rhymes with its translation, "Slowly, slowly."

We started this twenty-five-mile trek five days ago at the park entrance gate, at
6,000 feet, in air cool as clean sheets. We had thirty porters for our dirty dozen, each

THE HOROMBO COMPLEX OF HUTS AT 12,336 FEET ON THE HIGH SKIRT OF KILIMANJARO.

deftly balancing approximately forty pounds of gear and food atop his head, while we suffered along with headaches, day packs, and cameras. In the evenings they would cook up a storm, using camphor and podo wood collected around the brown, geometric A-frame huts built by the Norwegians in the early seventies. For our last hut, the cement-block Kibo, at 15,520 feet, well above any flowing streams, the porters also tote up our supply of fresh water.

As we make our way up the interminable hill we examine, in some continuing ritual, the faces of those loping down. Some are cadaverlike, some contorted, some an unadorned elegy of war and memory, and a few are blissful, eyes urging us to ask if they made the summit. A hearty woman from Tasmania we met at the first hut is barely recognizable as she passes us two days later, eyes suppurating, lips cracked, being braced down the mountain by two porters. Then, as we approach the Saddle, the long, red, windswept shoulder connecting the fraternal peaks of Kilimanjaro, Mawenzi and Kibo, two porters round the bend rolling a wheelbarrowlike stretcher with a dull-eyed European tucked inside. I suddenly picture myself in the same stretcher, violently ill with pulmonary edema. Daniel, our guide, asks the porters what happened to their patient. Somehow I feel better when Daniel translates that the young German fell out of his bunk in the Kibo Hut and broke his ankle.

Now I stop to look back down, and see the first pink flush of the African landscape spread beneath me. Unencumbered and flat, shiny as fresh paint, it is the floor of the Great Rift Valley. Just a week ago we were rambling along those steppes, looking at the wildlife that surrounds Kilimanjaro. The mountain creates water, and the water seeps to the plains, and supports all the megafauna of Africa, as well as the nomadic Masai. For five days we roamed around the base of Kilimanjaro in a dance of foreplay for the ascent. We pretended to enjoy the scenery, wildlife, and food (which fattened us for the sacrifice), but ever present, even when obscured by clouds, was the reason for our long journey to Africa: the isolated dome of Kilimanjaro.

I am higher than Mawenzi, the old, grim 17,564-foot peak seven miles away from the high cone of Kibo. It is messy and worn, as though composed of scrap dumped from some giant celestial chariot. Looking through an orange screen, between endless clouds thousands of feet below, I can see the curve of the earth for the first time. The sun appears, balanced on the central spire of Mawenzi, as if the volcano had spewed it whole from its long-dormant belly. A low-hanging halo of clouds between us reflects the rays down onto the snow-covered western

CAMPSITE AT THE FOOT OF KILIMANJARO. WE SPENT FIVE LAZY DAYS ENJOYING THE SCENERY, THE WILDLIFE, AND THE SUMPTUOUS FOOD, FATTENING OURSELVES FOR THE SACRIFICE OF THE CLIMB AHEAD.

face and over to Kibo. As the sun climbs, it looks like a hot-air balloon approaching the mountain.

I first saw Kilimanjaro ten years ago. I had been hired to assist in producing a television show, a segment for ABC's "American Sportsman" series. The concept was to take Sally Field, who had once been the Flying Nun on ABC, ballooning over Kilimanjaro. But when we arrived in Tanzania, we couldn't find the right grade of butane. The stuff we ended up with didn't allow a decent lift, so instead of Kilimanjaro, we did some meager ballooning across Ngorongoro and Lake Manyara. At one point the balloon crash-landed, knocking over a butane canister, which slammed into Sally's leg, cracking her patella. She left in a very bad mood. One of the cameramen, donning a wig, doubled as Sally for the rest of the shoot. And I never got to touch Kilimanjaro.

I'm onto my third tranquilizing play of the Bobby Brown tape. Then abruptly, at 6:33 A.M., we crest a ridge, and we're at Gilman's Point, 18,650 feet, the lowest spot along the almost perfectly circular, 1.2-mile-diameter crater. At least a dozen others are on this aerie, fellow *soi-disant* climbers and guides who started out before us. And suddenly all the Tanzanian guides break out into a jazzy, multiharmony song in Swahili, with a chorus of "Kili-man-jaro," which rings over the howling, icy air. This is where most climbers turn around. Of the 10,900 visitors to Kilimanjaro National Park last year, only about 5,000 made it to Gilman's; less than 2,000 continued around the crater rim to Uhuru Peak, the true and final summit.

I awoke in a hospital room, my body one massive ache. A doctor came in to visit me and said they had not been able to find the fistula with the angiogram, and so after I rested, they wanted to go in again. I asked what had caused this sudden condition, and he said nobody knew. It seemed to be a spontaneous incident. And if not plugged, paralysis was the usual outcome. Already, he said, there had likely been some permanent nerve damage, but they wanted to go in again and find this hole and cork it. He asked if I could feel anything in my left toe as he poked it, and I couldn't. He scheduled the next operation for the following morning, so I had a day to think about what life would be like without legs. This time I couldn't paper over my emotions. When Pamela came to visit, I broke down and cried uncontrollably.

There is nothing fake or stupid about this mountain. I can't fool it or myself. I couldn't stop at Gilman's and say I did the mountain, as so many do. Neither could my four companions. We are trapped by an inner honesty that didn't exist at lower climes. So off we go along a rib of broken rock, into a wind that cuts like a lie.

Things change for me at this point. I can no longer keep up with the team. Though we were told to breathe through our noses, retaining more precious moisture in our bodies, I simply can't do that. I suck air through my mouth, into constricted lungs. And I hear the racket of my breath, something I was told was a bad sign. The wind whispers *"pole, pole."* I have to downshift, and I remember advice Bill Broyles gave me the week

before departure. He had climbed the 23,036-foot-high Aconcagua, the tallest mountain in the western hemisphere, at age forty-two, a critical crossroads in his life between being editor-in-chief of *Newsweek* and executive producer of *China Beach*. He discovered the way to continue walking upward at altitude was to take a step and pause with the foot mid-air for a breather. I try the technique, but it doesn't seem to work. Instead I find if I take two steps, and then stop for several seconds of deep-dish breathing, I can then proceed, slowly—*pole, pole*—but surely.

THE GLACIERS NEAR THE SUMMIT ARE BIGGER THAN EVER. AT THIS ELEVATION, ICE DOES NOT MELT BUT SUBLIMATES AND TURNS IMMEDIATELY INTO WATER VAPOR. THE RESULT IS GLACIERS THAT LOOK VERY MUCH LIKE HUGE ICE CUBES SET ON A BUTTERCREAM-FROSTED CAKE.

The clouds are beginning to part, unveiling spires of blue ice and terraces of glaciers surrounding us, huge glaciers, bigger than hospital bills. I'm thankful Gary is right behind me, especially when he breaks the silence with an inspirational, "We're gonna make it now. Nothing can stop us." But then he coughs the dry cough of edema. Though Gary, too, has never been above 14,500 feet, he is an avid runner, hiker, weight trainer, and bicyclist. At fifty he is in the best shape of our team. Yet every time I stop for a breath, he stops as well, a commiserative shadow.

THE AUTHOR ON TOP OF UHURU
PEAK. THIS IS THE SHOW-
PIECE OF THE EXTINCT
VOLCANO CALLED
KILIMANJARO. *PHOTO BY
ROBERT FINNEY.*

I remind myself I am travelling with a round-trip ticket; that this is not Hemingway's awe-inspiring place of the dead, that we are beyond and above myth and illusion.

Again I awake in the hospital room. Across from me is another patient, an old man in extreme pain who rolls around and screams. When a nurse arrives he thinks she's his daughter, and blabbers incoherently about their family ties. I check my body, and though there is soreness from the operation, I feel okay. The pain in my legs is gone; I can move my feet, even wiggle my big toe. Yet there is no strength in my legs; they're like rubber when I swing around and plant them on the floor. A physical therapist helps me to the bathroom using a walker, and I think of what life will be like if this is my permanent condition.

My image of myself as an adventurer has broken up on the rocks of this ward. But the doctor finally pays his visit, and reports they still did not find the fistula, but believe it clogged itself, which sometimes happens though not very often. He thinks I should be able to walk in a few days, and that likely it will not return. There was some permanent nerve damage, which will mean a loss of some feeling in my big toe, but it shouldn't impair me. Why, in a few months, I could probably climb a mountain, he suggests. "Though be aware of any recurring symptoms," he says, "and get to a hospital if the pain or numbness spreads again beyond your toe."

Later, my family doctor dissents. "I'm not sure I agree," he says. "I think the sickness was related to you going to altitude after diving, something like the bends. I'm not sure if going up a mountain is the wisest thing to do."

Gary and I are alone on this mountain, animals in a space capsule. The other three disappeared over a rise about thirty minutes ago. Twice we see the summit, and muster the strength to make the last triumphant steps, only to see it roll away as though on wheels as we crest, revealing white scapes beyond that are higher still. So we continue trudging along, trying to react to the extraordinary scenery.

It's so close, but now I'm wondering if I can make it. My home is near the sea, where the oxygen density is more than twice that here. Does that mean I'm attempting this with the equivalent of one lung? I'm breathing like a chain smoker chasing a bus. I'm in the wrong skin for climbing. What can I do to keep going? The only reality is the mountain in my face. I can't cheat this one.

I keep on trekking.

Then we are there: top of the touchstone, the peak called Uhuru—Swahili for "freedom." The tiara of an extinct equatorial volcano, it is higher than any ground east of the Andes and west of the Himalayas. We step up to a shelf and become part of the sky. Daniel, our guide, is squatting by the sign that declares this the highest point in Africa. He's smoking a cigarette. A torn Tanzanian flag is wrapped tightly around a pole. "Congratulations. You made it!" I say to Dr. Steve, whose face looks like a gym bag. But then, nobody looks pretty here. "Yes, I did it!" the doctor exclaims, "I'm going to write up this combination of dexamethasone and Diamox. We can get grant monies to study this. This could be a breakthrough!"

I pull my camera from the inside of my jacket, and prepare to take a group shot, but the batteries are frozen. It is truly cold here, the wind violent in a strobelike way. Yesterday, knowing that my mind would be cloudy on top, I wrote a list of photos I wanted to take of gear that I used—my knife, watch, jacket, pack, and so on—but it is too cold to go through the exercise. Even Bob, the retired marine, who brought an American flag to unfurl on top, isn't able to dig it out.

Still, I have to have one shot. With the wobbly movements of an old man, I pull out my lap top computer, set it up, and ask Bob and Gary to take a few pictures with their cameras as I type away. Computing on top of Kilimanjaro; this would be my First.

Then I stand up and look around for a last time, faintly aware I am gazing at something terribly beautiful. And I wiggle my toe. It wiggles fine.

THE MOST VIOLENT ERUPTIONS ARISE FROM STEAM EXPLOSIONS, WHEN THE FIERY MAGMA REACHES SURFACE WATER OR GROUND-WATER. A DORMANT VOLCANO OFTEN EMITS STEAM AND MAY ERUPT AT ANY TIME.

It took an hour to reach a black-sand beach on the western side of Volcano Island, where we parked and off-loaded. Here I met Julio Sabit of Philvolcs (the Philippine Institute of Volcanology and Seismology), a sloe-eyed, nervous little man with apricot skin and a baseball cap. He would be my guide. We began the two-mile trek to Crater Lake, struggling up the slope of powdery volcanic ash. Julio told me the Philippine Government prohibits settlement on Volcano Island, which is a national park, but several thousand villagers eke out an illegal living raising ducks and growing corn, cassava, and upland rice in the rich volcanic soil, ignoring the seismic swarms that periodically shake the ground and remind that this is neither a safe nor permanent place. However, we didn't meet a soul as we swatted through the tangled vegetation and head-high grass for forty-five minutes, over gray tongues of sharp lava and still-steaming vents of recent eruptions. (Taal erupted every year from 1965 to 1970, then again in 1976, twice in 1977, and most recently in 1978. But, for the last couple of years there have been periods with great numbers of strong seismic tremors, sometimes as many as three hundred a day, suggesting another eruption is imminent). At last we crested the inner caldera ridge, marked by a small tamarind tree (all the large trees on Volcano Island were blown away in earlier eruptions). From this vantage we could stare one thousand feet down into the mouth of the volcano, into the apple-green waters of Crater Lake and the cork of an island that floats within. Even from here we could hear the ominous hissings of steam and gas, the sounds of violence.

Of the five hundred or so active volcanoes in the world, twenty-one are in the Philippines, a rattling string of some seven thousand worry-bead islands. And Taal, in the southern stretch of the main island of Luzon, may be the cruelest one of all, with the most eruptions and the highest cumulative body count.

A relatively new rival is Mount Pinatubo, just one hundred miles north, where I had been trekking just a few days before. It had erupted eighteen months earlier, in June of 1991, after six hundred years of sleep, in one of the most spectacular series of volcanic explosions this century. It ejected some ten billion cubic yards of sand, rock, pumice, and ash, deleting, as though with a computer keystroke, the top one thousand feet of the mountain. *Lahars*, rivers of volcanic ash mixed with rainwater and mud, whelmed down the mountain, burying some two dozen villages and over 200,000 acres of fertile farmland. By some estimates, nine hundred people died. The twenty megatons of ash and sulfur dioxide disgorged fifteen miles up into the sky continues to circle the world today, blocking sunlight, lowering global temperatures, depleting ozone, ending droughts, tipping stock markets, toppling governments and CEOs, and generally taking responsibility for every unexplained event in its wake.

As I hiked around the ash-gray, moon-like landscapes of Pinatubo, I crossed the remains of an

THE TAAL VOLCANO. FROM ITS OUTER RIM WE SEE THE CONE-SHAPED REMAINS OF A PEAK THAT PRE-HISTORICALLY SOARED 18,000 FEET ABOVE THE SEA.

entombed village called *Tabun* (which ironically, in the local language, means "to bury"). I stumbled over rooftops poking through dried mud; past a couch turned on end, with only the top two feet sticking out; the bare upper branches of once-tall trees; and the debris of human catastrophe—muddy clothes, melted phonograph records, and broken toys. Children with chalky faces were filling sacks with pumice to be sold for twenty cents and used to stone-wash denim jeans for export.

One of the Aetas, the nomadic, aboriginal tribe that lived on and around Pinatubo, stopped and asked, through a dirty handkerchief covering his mouth, for some relief money. When I gave him a few coins he explained that his people believe the spirits of their departed relatives live in the volcano, and are overseen by their god, Apo Namallari. Every year the Aetas made a pilgrimage to the caldera of Pinatubo to offer animal sacrifices to the sacred mountain and their god, and for centuries there was harmony, peace, and three harvests of rice a year. But when government geologists started geothermal drilling, to tap the inner energy of Pinatubo, Apo Namallari became angry and caused the eruption. Now forty thousand Aetas are homeless. But their cosmology is still intact, he maintained. They believe the declaration one survivor scrawled in red on a broken stucco wall: "We will return again."

It is a forty-five-minute trek across Volcano Island to Crater Lake, and along the way we step across the black and gray tongues of sharp lava—the dregs of recent eruptions.

Now I am deep within Pinatubo's fraternal volcano, the not-so-tall Taal (some say it is the lowest active volcano in the world), me and Julio down by the blast shards. I'm eating a sweet banana on a pyroclastic beach and wondering what to do. The

object of my desire is the little island in the lake, the final physical station, an improbable piece of real estate ringed in parrot-green vegetation. It looks alive, enticing, treacherous—a miniature version of Devil's Tower that has been well fertilized.

Dean Worster, an American biologist, who said he had been "lured by that strange impulse that so often leads people into foolish adventures," led an expedition to Taal's crater floor in 1888. Now I feel that same impulse as I strip to my shorts, and slip into the acid-tinged water of Crater Lake. It is bath-water warm, not at all uncomfortable, really almost sensual. The high mineral content, which includes boron, magnesium, aluminum, and sodium, makes swimming easier than in my pool. I swim several miles a week at home, so I'm not horribly intimidated by the distance of the task.

NEARLY 800 VOLCANOES ARE ACTIVE TODAY OR KNOWN TO HAVE BEEN ACTIVE IN THE PAST. OF THESE, MORE THAN 75 PERCENT ARE SITUATED IN THE PACIFIC RING OF FIRE. TAAL VOLCANO, ALSO KNOWN AS THE KILLER VOLCANO OF THE PHILLIPPINES, VENTS ITS STEAM FROM SMACK IN THE MIDDLE OF THE RING OF FIRE.

The first one hundred yards or so is fine; my skin isn't blistering or sloughing off, and I don't see any water boiling, which usually signals an imminent eruption. But then as I take a strong stroke some water splashes into my mouth. It's severe, sulfurous, salty and stings the back of my throat, like swallowing bees. I choke and cough, and question

THIS FISHERMAN MAKES HIS MORNING CATCH IN THE WATERS OF THE SOUTH CHINA SEA, WHICH SURROUND THE FRAGILE AREA.

the wisdom of this quest. I'm doing a dog paddle in the middle of one of the world's deadliest volcanoes. But I continue, now turning over to backstroke, thinking perhaps this will keep the water from my face. Nonetheless, as I move deeper into the lake, the waves grow bigger and slap at my head. I blink whenever a wave cuffs, but miss once and the water burns my eyes. This is like swimming through gastric juice.

In fact, I am swimming in diluted sulfuric acid. Acidity is measured by pH; the lower the pH, the stronger the acid. A neutral pH is 7. The pH of acid rain is as low as 4. Thomas Hargrove, the world's leading expert on Taal, had measured the pH of Crater Lake at 2.7, with about 3 percent sulphur. Well, at least I don't have to worry about poisonous snakes, because nothing can live in these waters. I turn and compare the distance I've come to where I'm headed, and guess I'm a third of the way there. For a moment I consider turning back, but then I hear the siren calls of uwaks, the dozens of crows that inhabit the hellish little island, and am compelled to continue.

It seems like hours, though it is less than one, when I reach the island, which is shaped like a basalt bathtub stopper. It is too steep to climb, so I pull myself up to an edged rock and lean back for a breather. There is an inexpressible vitality and exhilaration here: in the pungent smell of sulfur, in the sunshine on my face, in the beauty of the lunette-shaped destroyer itself. In the distance I can barely make out the round-faced figure of Julio, arms akimbo, impatiently awaiting my return.

It is incredibly exciting—and frightening—to be at the core of one of the earth's most powerful and destructive forces, aware that it could, and would, explode again and that I am tempting that fate. I feel the blood rush knowing my very existence is at the volcano's caprice. I have come to this domain uninvited, but I will leave only if it so wills.

This island didn't exist, nor did Crater Lake, in the beginning of 1911. The caldera surrounding me was then filled with mud, ash and two small pools of hot water, one green, the other almost red. Then, on the afternoon of January 29, 1911, this inner cone delivered a paroxysm that split the sky. Red balls of fire shot high above the crater. Day turned to night. Hot, suffocating gases filled the air. Blinding, choking sand and mud rained from the sky. And within minutes 1,335 people died. In terms of seismic intensity, it was the most powerful eruption ever recorded. And months later, when the dust cleared and the earthquakes subsided, there was a little island and a lake in the crater, a mote that still has no name.

Though I can't scale the island, I do manage to swim around to a point where a shiny, cabinet-sized box is drilled into the basalt. Julio told me this was a seismic monitor-transmitter that sends earthquake and eruption-predicting data via satellite directly to the University of Savoy in France, which in turn faxes the information back to Manila. I can't resist. Some sinister fancy possesses me. I reach up and give the box a few hearty raps, and it rings like the hollow barrel of a cannon. Might there be, I wonder, a fax making its way to Manila with my return swim?

And then I slide off the little green island into a lake in an island in a lake in an island in the sea, and head for the outermost ring, and the terra firma of my home near the San Andreas fault in California.

LIFE IS PRECIOUS IN THE SHADOW OF A VOLCANO, AND THOSE WHO LIVE THERE CELEBRATE IT AS SUCH, SOMETIMES DANCING INTO THE SUNSET.

All Nature is but art unknown to thee.
All chance, direction which thou canst not see.

—ALEXANDER POPE, 1733

SEEDS OF CHANCE:
THE PEAKS
OF MONTSERRAT

Joe O'Brien, the neighbor, forgot to water his cow, so the first sound of my first morning in Montserrat was a moo. The second was the tap-tapping of a hammer on a galvanized roof, the sound of construction, or in this case, reconstruction.

A bit of personal reconstruction is needed after twelve hours of flights and connections, so I put the pieces back together and swung out of bed. I could still smell the night-blooming jasmine as I crossed the loggia and inhaled the view: a garden with a dozen varieties of palms, with scarlet canna and bougainvillea the color of red lipstick, stretched to a sea that seemed clear enough to breathe. Less than three years ago some had pronounced this island dead in the wash of Hurricane Hugo, but there was nothing in these morning moments to indicate that. This place was alive and glistening.

Montserrat is a tiny island deep in the eastern Caribbean, a British colony with four-digit phone numbers, rental cars that look like golf carts, and no stoplights. There is nothing quite like it in the Caribbean, in the world. And yet I felt an affinity with the place. It had suffered a natural disaster of magnitude. On a mid-September Saturday night in 1989, Hurricane Hugo hit with 150-mile-per-hour winds, becom-

OLD PLANTATIONS AND THEIR GRAND ESTATE HOMES STILL DOT THE LAND-SCAPE OF "THE EMERALD ISLAND OF THE CARRIBBEAN."

ing the worst storm to hit the Caribbean in over a century. In its wake were ten dead, $400 million in damage, and nine of every ten homes a convertible. A little over two years later, on October 27, 1991, I was on the edge of another unbidden calamity—the Oakland Hills firestorm, the largest urban fire in U.S. history. It was a numbing blast of reality that suffocated whatever frail illusions of stability many had nurtured on this red-barked bluff overlooking San Francisco. The conflagration killed twenty-five people, destroyed more than three thousand homes, and blazed to within a block of my own. I was lucky, but every day as I drove past the barren landscape, the hollow plots, I couldn't help but stare and wonder. Where did everyone go? Why, after seven months, had no houses been rebuilt? Why were a third of the empty lots for sale? What happened to the once vibrant community just beyond my doorstep? Some of the answers had to do with bureaucracy, the stifling permit and building code systems, and the inhumanity of insurance companies who more often than not were offering insufficient payments for rebuilding. But what of the human spirit, the sheer will to overcome all obstacles and bounce back? In the natural order of things fire is often essential for the process of regeneration, but here it seemed an elegy to human loss.

So I wanted to travel to Montserrat and see if there was any connective tissue; to appraise this tropic analogue, and see how its people and environment fared. And this first look was quite nice.

But it was likely not representative. I was in the four-acre, million-dollar compound of Dr. Dean E. Burget and his wife, Undine. They were part of a wobbly ex-pat community that had built magnificent homes in the hills and on the scenic cliffs of the leeward side of the island. Many of these architectural wonders belonged to "snowbirds," wealthy Americans or Brits who would repair to the island during the winter months. Dean and Undine had lived here as residents for seven years, but were now thinking of moving on.

Though Dean was host for my little survey, I wanted to explore some of the backcountry to see how nature had fared after the blow, and Dean was not a hiker. So after a breakfast of sweet pineapple and papaya, I piled into the Toyota taxi of John Hickson, a big man in a big red shirt. The inside of his cab was like something out of a Jim Jarmusch film, with two air-fresheners cleverly disguised as eight balls dangling from the rear-view mirror and a rack of lacquered wooden beads draped over the driver's seat. We rumbled down the pocked roadway toward the capital, Plymouth, on the southwest coast. Seven years ago Dean Burget quit his practice as a plastic surgeon and moved to the Caribbean. With surgical precision he researched candidates for his new home, and settled on Montserrat. Why? Because it had no poisonous snakes, ample fresh water, charitable trade wind weather, and little crime, racial strife, or social unrest. And the best roads in the Caribbean. But no longer. Hugo had left a thousand ruts and holes, and John seemed determined to show off every one.

MOUNT CHANCE LOOKS DOWN ON THE DEVELOPMENT OF MONTSERRAT AND INTO THE
VIVID WATERS OF ISLE BAY.

Young dancers in front of the old sugar mill at Galway's Estate.

Along the way we passed an overlook where John pointed out the former location of Air Studios, the once state-of-the-art recording studio that gave Montserrat a moment of jet-set notoriety. Founded in 1979 by George Martin, the long-time Beatles producer, the facility had attracted a warehouse of music superstars, including Stevie Wonder; Phil Collins (and Genesis); Jimmy Buffett; Eddie Rabbitt; Air Supply; Duran Duran; Simply Red; The Police; Earth, Wind, and Fire; Black Sabbath; the Climax Blues Band; Dire Straits; and Mick Jagger and the Rolling Stones, who recorded their album *Steel Wheels* there. Montserrat was an ideal place to plop down and record an album, because of its notable lack of distractions (no discos, no casinos, no topless beaches, no neon, not even an all-night restaurant), and because the laid-back, low-key Montserratians didn't bother the stars, weren't impressed by their back-home reputations, and in most cases didn't know who they were.

But Air Studios is no more, blown away by Hugo as though in a Maxell tape commercial. And, as with many a dispute in the Oakland Hills, the insurance company wouldn't pony up enough to replace the facility, so the site remains silent. Some Montserratians miss the songs, and the money the rock stars brought; others feel the island was meant to be a quiet place, and thank Hugo as though he were a music critic with enough clout to close a bad show.

The so-called "Emerald Island of the Caribbean" (it was settled by the Irish in the mid-seventeenth century) looked green and luxuriant as we wound down the narrow breadfruit-lined road, no evidence of an apocalyptic hurricane in sight. In fact, there was little indication of any human habitation. There were more goats than people on the roadside. "How many live on the island?" I asked John. "About eleven thousand now, down about one thousand since before Hugo," he explained. It is also true that more Montserratians live overseas than on the island—

THE HALF-MILE-HIGH MOUNT CHANCE CREATES ITS OWN TROPICAL WEATHER, WHICH IN TURN ALLOWS A WONDERFULLY DIVERSE ARRAY OF VEGETATION, INCLUDING THESE RAINFOREST FERNS, TO FLOURISH.

some refugees from the Hurricane, but most seekers of better chances, a process that might be called reverse colonization. With little arable land and few natural resources,

CLIMBING IN THE HUMID MICROCLIMATE OF MOUNT CHANCE MAKES THE VETERAN GUIDES, EVEN ROGER PETERS, SWEAT UP A STORM.

there isn't much fat between the fur and the bones in Montserrat. About the only things locally made are sea-island cotton and postage stamps. In fact, the island's main source of income is monies sent home by overseas relatives, fueling a remittance economy.

Though the island is just twelve miles long, it takes almost twenty minutes to drive from the mid-island Anglo enclave of Woodlands to Plymouth, and it is like driving from the Oakland Hills to the Oakland docks: a fade to black, from fair to funky. While the homes of Woodlands were all restored to pre-Hugo perfection, many of the Plymouth knocks were yet to be mended. The washed-away wharf was in repair, the broken jetty was lined with a to-be-positioned pile of cement plugs. In downtown Plymouth, which looked a little down at the heel, most of the shops and Georgian-style buildings were restored and busy, yet a few skeletons stood, including the Montserrat Philatelic Bureau building, which sold the famous colorful stamps. Next to the crowded video store was a shop, not quite as popular, announcing: We Sell Brake Fluid, Pig Snout, Pig Tail. Just down the street, at the open market, all this was available, and more, the fitting backdrop for a dog that grabbed a goat's head from a stall and dashed across the street, a frantic woman in hot pursuit.

A bit farther down the street we passed the Bank of Montserrat, one of sixteen survivors of the 1989 Scotland Yard crackdown. Offshore finance was once seen as revenue manna from heaven, and was encouraged by Britain's Foreign and Commonwealth Office. In short order a golden horde of con-artists and scam merchants, plus stacks of funny money belonging to General Manuel Noriega, among others, poured in. At one time there was a bank for every forty inhabitants, some 350 to choose from, though most were little more than a fax number and a brass plate under a palm tree. Now, the offshore trade consists of a medical school and quickie weddings.

We continued south, beyond Plymouth, past Moose's Quick Fix Muffler Service, past the Yacht Club, which could boast not a single boat in anchorage, and along the construction site of a new seawall, to the cozy town of St. Patricks. Most of the towns and place names and even human names on Montserrat are of Irish origin, dating back to the mid-1600s when there were one thousand Irish families on board. Today not a single full-blooded Irishman lives here. The keepers of these names are of West African descent, imported as plantation slaves from the 1660s until 1834, when slavery

Looking down into the iron-oxide streaked ravine that is Galway's Soufriere.

was abolished. Now it's their island. On a roadside in St. Patricks we picked up our guide for the interior, the tall, thin Roger Peters, or Piggy, as he was known by his nickname. Every Montserratian has one.

Roger climbed in the back and directed us up a steep road that coiled inland into the mountains. Along the way he pointed out Galway's Estate, the remains of a slave plantation that was the island's largest for a time. Ten years ago it looked like Angkor Wat, buried in dirt and vegetation. But with the efforts of Lydia Pulsipher, a cultural geographer at the University of Tennessee, and teams of amateur archaeologists under her guidance, the caved-in sugar boiling house, the round turret of a wind-driven sugar mill, and the circular wall of a cattle-driven one have been partially restored. The site and its history are now featured as a case study in the Smithsonian's Seeds of Change exhibition, which celebrates the quincentennial of Columbus' New World landings, even though the intrepid sailor never stopped here. While passing by during his second voyage in 1493 the admiral noted that the little island with the serrated mountains reminded him of the terrain at an abbey called Montserrat near Barcelona. Of course, now that the grey stone ruins of David Galway's estate have been excavated there are plans to build an income-producing heritage center, a botanical garden, and a small hotel to help market the plantation as a tourist attraction. Some Montserratians, however, object to merchandising a monument to plantocracy, a reminder of the brutality of the slave era, and would prefer to see it fade like the memory of Hugo and other disasters.

When we reached the end of the road at last, John pinched his nose to the stench of sulphur and volunteered to stay with his taxi. So I took off with Pamela Roberson and Roger up the mountain notch into the surreal fumaroles of Galway's Soufriere, in the heart of an old volcano. We gingerly stepped along a crusty yellow path, beneath which we could hear the hissing and belching of superheated water, like the sounds of an unsettled stomach. We descended an iron-oxide-streaked embankment and crossed the White River, a hot springs creek that dribbled black water like oil, and Roger bent over to scoop up a drink. "Good for the body," he smiled, showing off a mouth with the discolored dentition of an extinct species. Then we climbed up the other side of the *ghaut* (the Amerindian term for "ravine") toward the Bamboo Forest. Across the valley was Chance's Peak, the highest point on Montserrat at 3,002 feet. Roger swept his hand toward its flanks. Hugo had sliced away every tree like a machete, he said, causing total ecocide. It had looked like Haiti, where the hills were deforested by a different natural disaster, man. Now, however, the forest was returning, and the flourishing hillsides were testimony to the recuperative powers of Nature. Roger also pointed out a glint of silver against the green, about 250 feet below the summit. It was a piece of wreckage, he said, from the September 17, 1965, crash of a Pan Am Boeing 707, flying from Martinique to Antigua in a morning storm. All twenty-one passengers and nine crew members died.

But from the thought of death we slipped into the life of the protected Bamboo Forest, an idyllic corridor of shadows and streams of light, filled with the quick movements and pleasant calls of the rare Montserrat oriole (*Icterus oberi*), the national bird. Known locally as the Tannia Bird, it is found no place else on earth. Half of its population of 1,200 was lost to Hugo, which erased a significant piece of the highland habitat. Nonetheless, the little bird has survived every cataclysm doled to the island with a chirp and a flit and a yellow breast puffed— a fitting symbol for the island.

Once through the Bamboo Forest, we were on a trail that meandered alternately through farmland and rainforest. This was a celestial path that would make Mo Siegel, founder of Celestial Seasonings, green. I gave it the pet name of The Tea Time Trail, as Roger pointed out the various plants that could be brewed or used as tisanes, including rum goat bush, awnie seed, trumpeter leaf, fever grass, Dominica weed, sweet mint, cat

DESPITE THE BEAUTY, TREKKING THROUGH THE HEART OF AN OLD VOLCANO IS UNSETTLING.

Negotiating the White River, a hot springs creek that boils through the surreal landscape of Galway's Soufriere, Roger Peters drinks from these waters and proclaims it is "good for the body."

mint, cinnamon tree, soursop leaves, strawberry leaves, rainfall leaves, mimosa leaves, baby ground nut, rock balsam, cattle tongue, lime leaves, and tamarind. Roger was a regular Euell Gibbons of Montserrat; when I asked him how Hugo had affected him, he replied that he'd lost his copy of *Back to Eden*, the classic Jethro Kloss book of natural edibles.

Roger had other talents as well. At one point we crossed a pass that allowed simultaneous views of the Caribbean and Atlantic waters; and Roger broke out into song: a Charlie Pride roundelay about snakes crawling, and sure enough in the middle of a chorus a black snake slithered across the path. This perhaps was not as allegorical as it seemed to me, because the mountain squirms with serpents. Nonetheless, I was impressed. Between yodels he'd take a toke on his Benson & Hedges and flash his gap-toothed grin. Roger is the island's premier C&W singer, and we got a private concert on the happy trail.

As we crested a hill that gave us a view of Antigua (twenty-seven miles to the northeast), Roger traced a line along a scape of elfin woodland. Some years ago a thriving community of over four hundred lived and farmed here. He even pointed out where the cricket field stood. But, by 1959 they all had left, seeking better fortunes. "What is the population of the island now?" Pamela asked, having missed my same inquiry of John a few hours before. "Right now it's down to about ten thousand five hundred and shrinking," Roger replied. That was a drop of five hundred since this morning, I thought. At this rate I'd have the island to myself by the end of the month.

The southern end of the trail brought us to the plantation of Sinclair Shoy, or Jahboca, his Rasta name. He was the leading christophene farmer on the island, a plant that reportedly brings down blood pressure, and it showed. Leaning against one of his five donkeys, with his basket hat rakishly floating on his dreadlocks, Jahboca couldn't have looked more relaxed. He rented his land for $100 per year from the Osborne Institute, grew string beans, cabbage, and anchobe (a breakfast vegetable served with salt fish), and he had a spectacular view of Guadeloupe, thirty miles to the southeast. The hurricane was a distant insult, and he was on with his life.

Back at St. Patricks we tanked up on Ting, a popular carbonated grapefruit drink that migrated, like the seventeenth-century Irish Catholic refugees, from Protestant St. Kitts. We were served by a bartender wearing a Chicago Bulls cap that remained forever pointed to a soap opera on the television, a show on one of the twenty-three stations available from Cable TV of Montserrat. Once slaked, we set out to tackle our next adventure, a hike to the island's most famous

ROGER PETERS IS A REGULAR EUELL GIBBONS OF THE ISLAND, A SELF-TAUGHT ETHNO-BOTANIST WHO CAN IDENTIFY EVERY PLANT AND ITS USE, BE IT MEDICINAL OR DECORATIVE. THE PLANT THAT LEAVES THIS WHITE IMPRESSION ON HIS ARM IS THE TATOO FERN (*PITYROGRIAMMA CALOMELANOS*).

natural attraction, Great Alps Falls. This time we bounced along in John's taxi to the southern end of the road, dodging goats and sheep along the way. We began trekking up the lower reaches of the White River, the same stream whose headwaters we had stepped across at Galway's Soufriere a few hours before. Again, Roger was a regular ethno-botanist, identifying every living thing that bloomed in the water-rich volcanic soil, from money and gum trees to the parasitic love vine, Mamee apple, mango, cashew nut, and almond trees; cocoa bean plants, mountain cherries, and soursops. No matter the economy, nobody goes hungry on Montserrat.

It was an easy forty-minute hike up to the falls, and in the canyon of the final approach I could feel the cool wind from the impending spectacle. The last bend was around a fifty-ton boulder that had been tossed to its present position from the base of the falls during Hugo's fury. Then we faced the Great Alps Falls. Though the seventy-foot-high cascade would not rank with the more elaborate versions in Dominica, Jamaica, and Cuba, they had a certain subtle beauty and charm, like much of Montserrat. I couldn't resist a shower, and stuck my head under the falls for a few minutes of heavy hydro-massage. Overwhelmed with the sensation, I found myself singing at top voice in the shower. When I emerged, Roger told me that I had bathed in the same falls as Boy George, Paul McCartney, Eric Clapton, and Sting, and that my singing was definitely the worst of the lot.

That evening I was invited to dine with the

FIVE WAYS TO QUENCH A THIRST AFTER CLIMBING A VOL-CANO IN THE TROPICS. THIS REFRESHMENT STAND IS IN PLYMOUTH, THE CAPITAL OF MONTSERRAT, ON THE SOUTHWEST COAST OF THIS TINY ISLAND IN THE EASTERN CARRIBEAN.

governor of Montserrat, His Excellency David G.P. Taylor, at the Edwardian Government House on Peebles Street. The grand white mansion, built in 1907 and decorated with a carved shamrock on its middle gable, seemed, on close inspection, chipped and faded, struggling for an antecedent dignity. The Queen's representative didn't have the gravitational pull of a colonialist with his over-laundered, wide-lapel, periwinkle blue shirt, brown loafers, rowdy helmet of hair, and Beefeater grin (perhaps that was an authentic appendage), and I

GREAT ALP FALLS IS THE ISLAND'S MOST FAMOUS NATURAL ATTRACTION. ITS WATERS HAVE WASHED OVER BOY GEORGE, PAUL MCCARTNEY, ERIC CLAPTON, AND STING.

had a hard time addressing him with the proper "Your Excellency." I think he felt a bit awkward as well, as he was not a career diplomat, but rather a Cambridge-educated businessman recruited by Margaret Thatcher to help put things back together in the Crown colony Falklands after the war. He did such a good job he was offered the governorship of Montserrat after Hugo, another clean-up situation. It was an anachronistic job, an unholy alliance, he admitted. There are only eleven British colonies left, and Hong Kong is about to go; Pitcairn is hardly worth the classification.

His Excellency's vision of the future of Montserrat lay in tourism, but of the small-scale, up-market variety. "We'll never attract or accommodate mass tourism," he explained, "and that's fine with me. I think we should concentrate on improving our services, our restaurants and hotels, hospitals, and in making the place tidier. To be truthful, I'm against the rock-star gimmick. And I can't see catering to the beach set. We have so few white beaches. Or the cruise set. We have no deep-water harbor. We have to be very careful about the quality and the number of people who come here. We need to preserve the scenery, charm and character of Montserrat." The problem with the governor's panegyric was all the lumpy and inconvenient statements coming out of the local government's office: plans for a longer runway at Blackburne Airport to handle bigger planes; schemes for three major resorts to more than double the current hotel room inventory; and blueprints for a $13-million seaport that would accommodate four-hundred-passenger cruise ships. Can the scenery, charm, and current character of a thirty-nine-square-mile mote co-exist with sixty thousand tourists, about twice the current number of annual visitors? Time will tell us.

As though contemplating this dialectic, the governor stared out into the mango tree, the national tree, on his manicured lawn. Then he closed his hand, making a fist, and said something that smacked of the kerosene-age colonial consciousness. He railed against television as though he were Jesse Helms critiquing the N.E.A.: "Television has rather corrupted the people here. They don't play cricket the way they used to. They'd rather watch the Bulls play. And, they now see things they shouldn't... nudity, drugs, violence. And they see things they don't have... fashionable clothing, makeup, VCRs... and they want them. They're no longer content." I could see His Excellency wasn't quite content either, as his philippic shifted to his distaste for the island's national dish, goat water ("nothing but Brown's soup with floating bits of bones and fat"), and for his lack of power ("in the Falklands I could make executive decisions, get things done; here I can only recommend"). Finally, as I left His Excellency I couldn't help but notice he looked as pale and weather worn as his old mansion, which he said the Foreign Office had promised to refurbish before his tenure was up in another year.

Back at Dr. Burget's house we lounged by the pool sipping a Perk's Punch (a locally brewed concoction of butter rum, pineapple, grapefruit juice, and a West Indian lime) listening to Pachelbel's Canon on the CD player and Dean on the Irish penny whistle, admiring the avant-garde Haitian art collection, and watching the stars. Here was the newest immigrant, separate, not equal, with little if any political power, but with the wherewithal to supply jobs in home construction, maintenance, and services. Not unlike the dynamics of the relationship between those in the precious homes of the Oakland Hills and those in the flatlands, or of the Santa Monica mountains and south central L.A. I talked with a realtor from Caribbee Agencies (which professes to offer Executive Properties on Montserrat), Gay Margun, a genteel woman with a diamond in her nose and seeming as if she didn't quite have twelve annas to the rupee. She specialized in fully furnished villa rentals, once a significant income earner for the island. The agency also offered homes for sale, but that business had not been booming, though the previous week she was proud to say a couple had seen a home listed at $400,000 in *The Robb Report* and called from their yacht to buy it unseen. She explained that beginning in 1962, the government decided to divide certain scenic plots of land into "beachettes," and sell them off to foreigners. Since the island was known as a quiet, stable place, it attracted a number of middle-aged and older Americans looking for a retirement or second home,

and realtors grazed prosperously off these dreams. Now, however, these original homeowners are advanced in years and concerned about health facilities. It's clear open-heart surgery won't be available for a while, so many of the pioneers are selling and moving on. And there isn't a full suitcase of newcomers calling. Many are cautious in the aftermath of Hugo. Others just don't have the cash the way an earlier generation did. So the neo-colonist realty business is a tough one.

THE EDWARDIAN GOVERNMENT HOUSE, BUILT IN 1907 ON PEEBLES STREET, WHERE THE UNION JACK FLAPS OVER ONE OF THE REMAINING ELEVEN BRITISH COLONIES.

The following day I had hoped to climb Mount Chance for a crow's-nest look at the entire island, but as usual, the mountain was camouflaged by clouds, and the air felt clogged and granular from the fine Sahara dust swept across the Atlantic. So, I decided to tour the island instead. First I wandered down the street from The Vue Pointe Hotel, past a realty company called ASDIP (another shitty day in paradise?), down to a nondescript, suburban-type home with a For Sale sign out front listed by Caribbee Realty. It was the home of Paula Dutcher, the "Dragon Lady." Every morning at 9:00 she would step out to her backyard on the edge of a cliff and hand-feed Miss Iggy, Fella, Miss Gimpy, and the others. Before Hugo, only a handful would visit her breakfast table, but now upwards of fifty iguanas crawled over each morning. I sat back in awe as iguanas emerged from the ocean cliff, looking as though they were evolving in front of me, slithering from sea to land and Paula's outstretched hand. She merrily fed her pink-mouthed tribe, first with hibiscus, then mango, papaya, soursop, and finally, the piece de resistance, Wonder Bread, the runaway favorite. I asked Paula who would take care of the iguanas when she moved, and she said she wouldn't sell unless she was convinced the new owners would tend to the brood as she had. And it involved more than just daily feedings. Iguanas are a popular food for Montserratians, and more than once she's had to chase away local would-be gourmands.

Next I visited the Bird Sanctuary at Foxes Bay. It was a place that reverberated with sounds, like being on hold with Banana Republic—though I didn't actually see anything more exotic than green herons and cattle egrets. The forest and manmade structures were levelled by Hugo, and for a time the Bay lived up to the marketing tag the island uses: "The way the Caribbean used to be." For over two years the bay probably would have been recognizable to Ciboneys, Arawaks, and Carib Indians, who called the island *Alliouagana*, meaning "land of the prickly bush." But the mangroves and manchineel trees had come back, and some members of the Montserrat Rotary Club were busy pounding nails into a new pavilion and concession stand. There were a few bathers on the black-sand beach. The phoenix was rising.

For lunch I wandered down to a popular liming spot, The Nest. Over a twelve-ounce Red Stripe (Jamaica's finest beer) I met Danny Sweeney, a potbellied sportsman whose claims to fame were that he had taught Sting to windsurf and that he'd won the annual fishing tournament. Danny was all good cheer, until there was a commotion on the beach, and a crew dragged a sixty-pound kingfish to the parking lot. It was a record catch for that beach, and a crowd surrounded the team, taking photos. Danny shoe-horned between shoulders and jested, in a Willy Loman sort of way, "Take a photo o' me, mon. I won the tournament."

I also ran into a couple who had won a game show in London called *Blind Date*, a British version of *The Dating Game*. Their prize was a long weekend in Montserrat accompanied by a video crew, who would present an edited version of their dream date on an upcoming show. The only problem was they didn't like each other. He was too short, she declared hotly. He just shrugged. But they both said they were gamely going through the exercise, and were glad the show gave them separate rooms. I also met a young couple from Denver who was in the middle of an extended Caribbean island hop, stopping off just about every place LIAT (Leeward Islands Air Transport) could land its Dash 8's. They told me they had planned this trip a year ago and had written to the tourist boards of thirty-five islands requesting information. Thirty-four replied. The only hold out: Montserrat, whom they had written twice. Yet, despite its reluctance to accommodate tourists, or perhaps because of such, Montserrat was, in the opinion of the Denver couple, the most pleasing stop of their journey: the least pretentious, the most compulsively friendly, and the most physically attractive. They confessed they were thinking of moving to Montserrat.

By day's end, the sky had cleared and Chance's Peak seemed to sip light from the sun. I made a vow to make the hike no matter the conditions the next morning, and

called Roger to see if he would be my guide. I was hungry from a busy day, and knew tomorrow was going to be an energy-expensive exercise, so I was looking forward to a solid meal. Mountain chicken seemed the ticket. The popular dish is actually a large, meaty frog that lives on the flanks of Mount Chance, and the Blue Dolphin Restaurant is the prime purveyor of the exotic dish.

ROSE WILLOCK, M.B.E., THE GENERAL MANAGER OF RADIO MONTSERRAT, STEPS UP A MISTY MOUNT CHANCE.

We walked into the modest restaurant to the sight and sound of Irish pop singer Van Morrison on the television. My party, consisting of Pamela and the Burgets, was the only one in the place, so after we placed the order I felt it would not be much of an interference to wander back and visit the cook, Simon Meade. Simon, who said he doesn't eat mountain chicken because of allergies, explained that his suppliers would hike up the skirt of Mount Chance after dark, and with a flambeau (a beer bottle filled with kerosene—cheaper than a flashlight) seek out the giant frogs. Once they got back to Simon, he'd cut off the drumstick-sized legs, marinate them in a spicy red sauce, dip them in flour, then egg wash, then bread crumbs, and drop them into the frying pan. They were delectable, yet I couldn't help but feel a pang of guilt as with each bite I heard a chorus of "ribbits" just outside the window.

The best time to climb Chance's Peak is early morning, before the weather sets in, so I picked up a dairy-fresh Roger at 7:00 A.M. But upon arrival he said I might be too late. For most Montserratians this is practically midday, but I was still sloughing off jet lag: 7:00 A.M. in Montserrat was 4:00 A.M. in Oakland. With Roger was Rose Willock, M.B.E., the general manager of Radio Montserrat (AM 88.5), who had climbed Chance's

Peak fifteen years ago as a schoolgirl, and now wanted to do a radio show update. Rose was a ball of energy, always broadcasting something, so buoyant I got the impression that if she stepped off a cliff she would fall up.

In an underpowered Toyota we sputtered up a steep road paved with so many little yellow impatiens they looked like continuing constellations. At the trailhead, we parked, shouldered our backpacks, and headed up the…stairs. This was the first surprise. The last time Rose made this trek it was an all-day expedition, plodding up a muddy embankment. But after Hugo, Cable & Wireless (West Indies) decided to put in steps to make the pilgrimage to their digital microwave radio tower on top easier. Now it was two thousand wooden-framed steps to the summit, the ultimate Stairmaster.

When we started it was a gorgeous day, and we could clearly see our goal, could almost taste the top. But things change. As we rested on a platform at about 834 steps, I watched clouds paw the cone-shaped stone towers below us, the remains of two-hundred-year-old sugar mills and the only high rises on the island. Then the mist spun, wrapping its damp hands around us. I took a moment to tell Rose I had been looking for analogies between the firestorm that had razed my neighborhood and the wrath of Hugo, and comparisons in how victims dealt with the aftermath. Rose bent over in laughter, and then chastised me in her lyrical brogue for the thought. "There is no comparison between your crucible and ours. Fire is so much worse…it obliterates everything. And the people of Oakland owned so many things. By contrast, we didn't lose much; we didn't have much to lose. We lost roofs. We lost windows and doors. We lost some furniture and stuff, that's true, but we never lost the most important thing to us: our sense of humor. And what did go that was material, we knew we could replace or rebuild. Everyone became a carpenter after Hugo. And we're still bringing it back. But we didn't have to deal with a fire that took away everything. We were battered, but not burned to a crisp. Your neighbors really had it much, much worse."

The cloud seemed to tighten its grip with Rose's reflexive sermon, and I turned to follow her voice as she started upwards. I was a bit startled by her response to my inquiry, but she was probably right. Perhaps more telling, though, was her attitude. It wasn't one of a victim empathizing with another's plight. It was the spirit of someone who would continue climbing through cloacal muck without a whine or word of protest, regardless the weather, no matter the steepness. Hers was some Gaian spirit, the earth rebounding without even a sigh after every indignity. I wanted to tell her this, but she disappeared into the fog. Not to worry; ever the communicator, Rose sent me various forest faxes along the trail. I'd look down and see a big heliconia leaf resting on a step, with a message scrawled in pen: "I'm just ahead, and waiting…Rose"

Finally, I made the crowning steps to Triangulation Point, the highest point on Montserrat. And I couldn't see a thing. The trees embowered, the clouds enshrouded and let loose a cold rain. A short ways down the other side I found Chance's Pond, where legend has it a mermaid lives with a golden comb, which if stolen will make the robber

rich. Yet the pond looked like a small swamp, and there was certainly no sign of a mermaid, or even Rose, who summited the peak, then promptly headed back down in front of Roger and me.

And so I stood on the top, the midst of a microclimate, and looked around at nothingness. In the fog everything was luminous, but nothing clear. I realized decoding Montserrat was like holding a mirror to a mirage. I really had no idea

THERE ARE NO DISCOS, NO NEON, NO CASINOS ON MONTSERRAT—JUST THE HOMEMADE COSTUMES OF A CHRISTMAS DANCER ON A BLACK BEACH THAT RIMS THE ISLAND.

why or how the people of this volcanic isle, the trees and the plants, had rebounded with such apparent ease. It was not a good idea to think there might be an Oakland-Montserrat ecumenicalism, to believe that I could reimagine the universe from the vantage of Chance's Peak. But I sensed there was a spirit here, the soul of a Roger or a Rose, that was affirmative, inquisitive, creative, and ready to move onwards and upwards. Regardless the wind, whatever the view.

Now, as I type on my computer at home in the Oakland Hills, on a ridge that could be called Second Chance, I look out over a disaster zone, the vacant lots that were once homes filled with the flux and clatter of families. I can see a FOR SALE sign, but I also see a blanket of bright, tangerine California poppies scattered over most of the burned area. And I can hear the tap tapping, the sounds of reconstruction.

Mehemea ka tuoho ahau me maunga tei tei. (If I should bow my head, let it be to a high mountain.)

—Maori proverb

MOUNT COOK:
PIERCING CLOUDS
FROM BOTH SIDES NOW

When the Sherpas of Nepal celebrate an anniversary, they burn butter candles as votive offerings to the gods. Personally, I've never lit any light to mark an anniversary, never even raised a glass in a reminiscent toast. In an age when the future unfolds so fast it takes full attention to climb aboard, anniversaries dwell too much on an obliterated past.

Nineteen ninety-three was a big year for anniversaries. It was the 400th birthday of Izaak Walton; the 250th of Thomas Jefferson; the 100th of Cole Porter. It was the 30th anniversary of JFK's assassination. It was 40 years ago James Watson and Francis Crick deciphered the structure of DNA. It was the 25th anniversary of Otis Redding's "Sittin' on the Dock of the Bay"; of Bob Dylan's album, *John Wesley Harding*; of the premiere of *60 Minutes*; of *2001: A Space Odyssey.* Thirty years ago the first woman, Valentina Tereshkova, rocketed into space. It was the 50th anniversary of the invention of SCUBA by oceanographer Jacques Cousteau. Five hundred and one years earlier Columbus "discovered" the New World. Mount Whitney was first climbed 120 years ago; Mount McKinley eighty years ago. And forty years ago, during the same week Queen Elizabeth II was coronated, a lanky, thirty-three-year-old New Zealand beekeeper reached the angular summit of Mount Everest, the world's highest peak, and became an icon of global consciousness.

ONLY ONE ROAD ENTERS AND LEAVES THE PARK.

MOUNT COOK IS THE CROWN OF THIS SEISMICALLY ACTIVE AREA.

The year 1993 was studded with anniversary celebrations for Sir Edmund Hillary and his living climbing companions. There was an enormous fete in London, at the Royal Geographical Society, attended by Queen Elizabeth, Lord John Hunt (the leader of that epic 1953 expedition), and the elite of the expedition set. There were anniversary treks in Nepal, fund-raisers in San Francisco, documentaries in Auckland, articles that came dangerously close to hagiography, and a dizzying parade of congratulatory dinners. "I'm getting pretty tired of the circus," Ed told me when I called him in Auckland in June.

So, while all the attention was lavished on Ed's crowning achievement, and thousands flocked to Nepal to trek in his footsteps, and a record forty people summited Everest on a bright day in May, I thought I would look back in a different way. I decided to travel to Mount Cook (12,284 feet), on the South Island of New Zealand, where Ed cut his eyeteeth as a climber. I went to shamble solo up a route he pioneered, the South Ridge of the Cook massif, back when he was an unknown outdoor enthusiast. I would quietly follow in the Big Man's bootsteps in a different way than the madding crowd. Furthermore, I thought I would do it in June, which is midwinter in New Zealand, to ensure my solitude. Long before Ed became world famous he was a young Auckland air navigator who would use his spare time to slip away and make solo expeditions, often in

June, because he found winter climbing greatly to his taste. Of no significance was the fact that this was the seventieth anniversary of the first winter ascent of Mount Cook.

I arrived at the Hermitage Hotel, a half mile high at the base of Mount Cook— the same hotel out of which Ed based in February 1948 when he made his assault on the South Ridge. I was a bit dismayed when I stopped in the visitor center on the way to the hotel. I noticed that Mount Cook National Park, the 173,000 acres at the end of a road that follows the shore of Lake Pukaki, was officially established in 1953, so this spot, along with Ed's Everest climb, was celebrating its fortieth anniversary. But the concierge said he knew of no festivities planned and, in fact, things were quieter than ever. The Hermitage holds some three hundred beds, yet there were just a dozen guests, along with the sixty staff members, on the property.

Outside the sun was aestival, yet the snow-laden landscape looked brutally brumal, like a northern European Christmas setting. I could see the icy wedge of Mount Cook from my frosted window, and the dead-white summit itself, that little patch of snow where all the ridge lines meet.

AFTER HIKING UP THE WEST BANK OF LAKE PUKAKI INTO THE BOSOM OF MOUNT COOK IN 1862, JULIUS VON HAAST WROTE, "NOTHING I HAVE PREVIOUSLY SEEN CAN BE COMPARED WITH THE SCENERY, WHICH CERTAINLY HAS NOT ITS EQUAL IN THE EUROPEAN ALPS."

There are New Zealanders who have been to Mount Cook a score of times and never seen the tent-shaped roof of their country, so I felt lucky to have this large slice of good weather, and was anxious to get outside. After a shower and a meat pie, I wandered over to Alpine Guides, the best in the park, and went over my plans. Bryan Carter, who was celebrating his twentieth anniversary with Alpine Guides, was not keen on my plan to make a solo hike up to the Hooker Glacier, the route Ed used to make his ascent. The trail was unmarked in the deep snow, and this was the height of avalanche season. "You can make it to the lake, but don't go any farther. Definitely don't try to make the Hooker Hut," he warned. With those words I retreated to the local sop for thirsty adventurers: the Tavern Bar in the Hermitage, where I spent the afternoon and evening exploring the contour lines of frosted glasses and peanut bowls.

The next morning my breakfast was a breath of fresh air and a good look around. I pulled on a pair of long underwear, struggled into my Gortex expedition suit, and wrapped it all in a hefty down jacket, before stepping from the reasonable into the

ON MAPS IT IS MOUNT COOK, THE TALLEST MOUNTAIN IN THE SOUTHERN ALPS. TO THE MAORIS IT IS AORANGI, OR CLOUD PIERCER.

extreme. The air beyond the hotel door was so cold it fizzed and snapped; every breath I took seemed to cut my throat. Fresh snow coated the landscape. Just off the hotel terrace, a sign marked the way to the Hooker Valley Track, and I followed its direction across the tufted flats toward the low moraines east of White Horse Hill. In a short time I passed

the site of the original Hermitage, a simple cob-wall cottage built in 1884 and destroyed in a flash flood in 1913. (The eightieth anniversary of a disaster.)

For the next thirty minutes, though I was surrounded by powerful peaks, I couldn't see the pyramidal mountain I had come to see. On my left I passed the stone Alpine Memorial, dedicated to Londoner Sydney King and local guides Darby Thomson and Jock Richmond, who were swept away by an avalanche in 1914 and became

THE ENTRANCE TO MOUNT COOK NATIONAL PARK, THE 173,000 ACRES SURROUNDING THE NAMESAKE MOUNTAIN THAT WAS ESTABLISHED THE SAME YEAR EDMUND HILLARY CLIMBED MOUNT EVEREST.

the first of many climbers to die on Mount Cook. I didn't stop, and instead picked up the pace as I passed through broken hummocky hills walled by the low lines of morainic boulders. These moraines are the marks of different phases of glacier advance and retreat, which even in recent times have greatly altered the landscape. Gone is the arch beneath 100-foot-high ice cliffs spread across the snout of the Mueller Glacier, which greeted gold-seeker Julius von Haast when he wandered into this vault of nature in 1862. (He was so impressed, he named the valley and its main glacier after the distinguished botanist of the day, Sir William J. Hooker.) Gone, too, is the ice bridge over the Hooker River, which, before 1900, enabled merino sheep from Birch Hill Run to be put to summer pasture on the upper Hooker flats. And Te Waewaw Glacier above Stocking Stream

THE JULY WINTER TURNS THE TUSSOCK AND TURPEN-TINE SCRUB INTO LONG, CURVED ICY FINGERS.

no longer looks like a stocking; its foot and lower leg have been unravelled by ice retreat.

I came to a bridge constructed of four cables stretched some forty feet across and suspended fifteen feet above the daunting drainage of the Cook massif. The bottom two cables supported a wire mesh walkway, while the upper pair served as handrails. I wobbled and bounced across, keeping a wary eye on the rushing, glacial waters below that threw a blast of refrigerated air my way. Once across, I turned back and looked down the valley across to the hotel's backdrop—the Sealy Range. There, amidst the serrated skyline, was the undistinguished Mount Olivier, the first real mountain Ed Hillary climbed as a young lad on a short vacation in 1939. The impetuous and kinetic Hillary dashed to its summit, leaving in the dust the mountain guide he had hired. "It was the happiest day I had ever spent," he later said.

Just before the second swing bridge, I passed a shingle cliff festooned with icicles and snapped one off to suck on as I walked. Halfway across the bridge I stopped and grabbed the railings tightly. An ominous crack resounded, and rolled into a deep rumble. I looked around in time to see a puff and then a slow cascade of white: an avalanche crashing down the eastern wall of Mount Sefton. At 10,355 feet, it is a little smaller than Mount Cook, but just as dangerous. From here it was just half a head turn away.

Once across the bridge, I tramped up the valley, and turned a corner. Suddenly, the perfect pyramid of Mount Cook, permanently coiffed in snow and ice, burst into sight—just as it had to Ed forty-five years ago, and to the Maoris well before him.

The Maoris, who arrived in New Zealand a couple of hundred years before the Europeans, called it Aorangi, or Cloud Piercer. It was officially named Mount Cook in 1851, after the great Yorkshire navigator, who never even saw his namesake. It was christened by Captain J.L. Stokes of the H.M.S. *Acheron,* who spied the peak while sailing down the west coast. At 12,284 feet (formerly 12,349 feet), Mount Cook is the tallest mountain in New Zealand, and Australia for that matter. But Cook is only one of more than twenty-five ice-draped peaks above 10,000 feet in the Southern Alps, the sharp spine of mountain country that runs the length of the South Island.

In this unique region, the land rises so quickly that the two-mile-high peaks are within twenty miles of the sea. The steep terrain, combined with the heavy rains of the southern latitudes known as the Roaring Forties, have created hundreds of glaciers. Nowhere else on earth are there so many glaciers at so low an altitude, and I was heading toward one—the Hooker. This, like the other glaciers here, was created by the vast precipitation (as much as three hundred inches a year) that falls in its névé, or head and slowly compresses to form blue-tinted, oxygen-rich ice that flows downhill under its own weight. But the Maoris have a more lyrical explanation. To them this river of ice is Ka Koimata o Hinehukatere, or The Tears of

IT WAS IN THE AREA THAT IS NOW MOUNT COOK NATIONAL PARK.THAT THE YOUTHFUL EDMUND HILLARY MADE HIS FIRST CLIMB UP AN INNOCU-OUS PEAK IN 1939.

A SHEEP DOG KEEPS HIS FLOCK UNDER CONTROL IN THE SHADOW OF MOUNT COOK.

THE GREY BRAIDS OF THE UPPER TASMAN RIVER DRAINING MOUNT COOK. THE CLOUDY
WATER CONTAINS FINE SUSPENDED ROCK FLOUR, WHICH IS CREATED BY THE
TASMAN GLACIER AS IT GRINDS AGAINST THE BEDROCK.

the Avalanche Girl. Hinehukatere and her lover, Tawa, who hated the mountains, were climbing high one day when he slipped and was lost. She cries to this day, and her tears freeze to form the glacier.

THE MOUNTAIN WAS NAMED IN 1851 AFTER THE GREAT YORKSHIRE NAVIGATOR, WHO NEVER EVEN SAW HIS NAMESAKE.

Hillary probably didn't care too much about the myths, or about anniversaries, when he approached this sea of ruptured ice. His mind was focused on higher ground. Mountains were there to be climbed and climb them he would, without the frills.

This is a seismically active area, an area of continuous mountain building at the margins of the Pacific and Indo-Australian plates. But the brooding peak filling this valley was not any higher than when Ed was here; in fact, it was appreciably smaller. A little after midnight on December 14, 1991, the top of Mount Cook collapsed in an enormous rock avalanche down the East Face. About fifty-five million cubic yards of rock and snow plummeted down a fifty-seven-degree slope, travelling at two hundred to three hundred miles per hour for over four miles and missing several climbing parties, asleep in the Plateau Hut, by less than a thousand feet. The great mountain was now sixty-five feet shorter. It was getting closer to Mount Tasman, New Zealand's second highest peak at 11,475 feet.

Which brings to mind another controversy. Suppose Mount Everest turned out *not* to be the highest spot on the planet, but Pakistan's K2 were higher? For years scientists

Nowhere else on earth are there so many glaciers at so low an altitude.

have debated the respective heights, now officially 29,022.6 feet for Everest and 28,268 feet for K2. On a 1986 expedition, after measuring electromagnetic signals from a satellite, Seattle astronomer George Wallerstein calculated K2 had an elevation of 29,064 feet, a few feet above Everest's high point. If Everest is indeed the king, as the latest laser survey suggests, what if an avalanche brought down the top a few hundred feet, and K2 emerged supreme? Where would that leave Edmund Hillary in the history books? What would become of the whole romantic narrative of mountaineering? Can anyone—outside of alpine enthusiasts—name the men who first climbed K2, which is considered the tougher challenge, regardless of height? (They were Italians Achille Compagnoni and Lino Lacedelli, who reached the steep summit of gleaming ice that straddles the Sino-Pakistan border July 31, 1954.)

In the week before Christmas in 1988 I found myself in New Delhi sharing dinner with Ed and his wife, June. He was serving a term as the New Zealand ambassador to India, Nepal, and Bangladesh, a seemingly unlikely job for a mountain climber. But no Westerner was more revered in these parts and when he spoke, half a world listened. I gave him a book I had written a few years back about rivers down which I had made the exploratory descents on, geographical firsts in some ways not unlike his own. (A tough river never before navigated was often called "the Mount Everest of rivers" by river rats.)

Rivers, though, have never offered the linear purity of mountains, and since they are ever moving,
there's no there there. Not surprisingly, no water-
way has ever captured the world's imagination in
the same way Everest has. Beyond that, I could

A FULL WINTER MOON RISES
OVER THE SOUTHERN
ALPS.

never pretend to equate my wanderings with Ed's crowning feat. Yet, just when I wanted
to ask him how he ended up on top of the world, he paused, turning his attention from
his lamb curry, and asked, "Why you? Why were you, of all the river runners around, the
first to negotiate these rivers?"

"It was just luck. It could have been anyone. I was at the right place at the right
time," I answered.

Ed understood. He knew about luck. He knew how easily someone else's name
could have entered the pantheon of knighted heroes. He knew the good weather was a
roll of the dice that went his way, and that even from a publicity standpoint, his timing
couldn't have been more perfect—the news of his success reached England the night
before the coronation of Elizabeth II, a convergence of triumph for a fading empire. Ed
never claimed to be the world's greatest climber, he was just the first white man on the
highest. And yet, unlike many who have had greatness thrust upon them, his life didn't
go downhill after his peak experience. He returned to the Himalayas again and again, in
a less glamorous fashion, to help the Sherpa people build schools, hospitals, bridges,

freshwater pipelines and to participate in reforestation projects. This is Edmund Hillary's greatest triumph.

I continued the hike through flats and terraces, in an area I knew was splashed with the colors of the Mount Cook lily (the largest ranunculus in the world) and other wildflowers in early summer. Now, in June, there were only spectral whites and mournful grays. I followed the tracks of an unknown cross-country skier who had followed the Hooker River, milky from the rock flour ground by the glacier. Ed himself had skied up the Hooker, around this same date, back in 1949, so I guess this skier was making a forty-fourth anniversary run. As I got closer, I could hear the glacier talking to itself in loud cracks and gurgles. I looked up. With the dramatically symmetrical Mount Cook in my gaze, and dozens of shimmering high mountains enveloping me, I felt as if I were in an alien, beautiful world.

My sense of scale was lost. This was just too immense, too awesome for the brain to properly process. Mount Cook's spectacularly creased peak looked like it was a stone's throw away. The Hooker Glacier stretched in front of me like the frozen river it is, part of it studded with ice pillars, some of it smooth and sparkling in the sun, and some swept into stiff peaks and ridges, looking as if someone had taken a pogo stick through a field of meringue. I could see the wind spinning snow off Mount Sefton. At first I thought it was another avalanche, but it made no sound, and it didn't let up. I realized that the effect was created by a high and powerful wind, one the villagers call a "nor'wester."

I proceeded through the ever-deepening snow until I reached the terminal lake. This was the point at which I was to turn back. The skinny ski tracks I had seen on the trail did an abrupt 180 here. A park service sign warned: AVALANCHE ZONE! HAZARDOUS ROUTE AHEAD. TRACK CLOSED BEYOND HOOKER TERMINAL LAKE DUE TO AVALANCHE DANGER. Ed had encountered similar warning signs back in 1948, though they were unwritten. But he didn't turn back. Not here, not on Everest. I, too, ploughed on.

Since the lake was frozen, I figured its surface would be the easiest route across. I stepped onto its frozen surface. Treading lightly along the glaze, I made good progress. I was about halfway up the length of the lake when I heard a sound like shattering glass. I looked down and saw a web of cracks appear around my boots. I gingerly took another step. The ice began to indent as more wrinkles appeared on the surface. The water beneath the ice emitted a dull, digestive growl. This would not do. Alone and in midwinter, I couldn't afford to fall into a glacial lake. I inched back and over to the lateral moraine shore and scrambled up a scree slope, slipping back a foot for every three upward. Consisting chiefly of sedimentary rock called greywackle—hard sandstone and siltstone about 200 million years old—Mount Cook was not built to last. Kiwis call this stuff I was trying to scale "Weet-Bix," after a popular breakfast cereal with about the same texture, strength, and, Kellogg's might say, taste.

I paused at a long, crooked crease in the snow. Perhaps it was the trail. It was impossible to tell with certainty because the snow was a couple of feet deep. But every

THE NEVE OF THE TASMAN GLACIER. THIS IS THE LARGEST AND LONGEST GLACIER IN NEW ZEALAND.

fifty yards or so was a marker, either a stone cairn or a five-foot-high metal bar, sticking out jaggedly, like broken bones through skin. Using these markers as guides, I slowly hoisted myself up into the impressive but forbidding wasteland.

Soon I was beyond the lake, in the Ablation Zone, adjacent to the Hooker. I stepped onto the pleats of the mountain's skirt. The glacier looked to be less than a hundred feet deep where its liquid runoff melted into the gray lake, but upstream I knew it was almost a thousand feet thick and a quarter mile wide in places. The Empress, Noeline, and Mona glaciers, pushing down from Endeavor Col (named for Captain Cook's ship) on the Mount Cook Range, all swing southward, combining into one great ice fall—the short, steep, and thick Hooker Glacier.

It was at the head of the Hooker that Ed had first proved some of his mountaineering mettle. Just three days after his successful climb of the South Ridge, he was off again, this time with a group, up beyond the glacier's head. When one of his climbing partners, Ruth Adams, slipped and fell sixty feet, Hillary stayed with her while others went for help. With terrific energy he hacked out an ice cave six by four by four feet, breaking his ice ax in the process. He nursed along the badly injured Ms. Adams for twelve hours, until 10 P.M. that night, when one of the rescuers showed with a sleeping bag. It took another week to get her off the mountain. (Ruth Adams sur-

LAKE PUKAKI, AT THE TERMINUS OF THE TASMAN RIVER, REFLECTS THE BLUE SKY.

vived, and went on to become a respected doctor.)

I continued to wade through the snow, each leg movement a ritualistic gesture, like a benediction without a recipient. Then a silence overtook me at once. It was so total my ears roared...or was that another avalanche? Then I saw blood. The footprints of a European hare ran parallel to my own for a good thirty yards, and then ended at a sprawled mark in the snow soaked with red stains. A harrier hawk? The haunting, ravenlike native morepork? The New Zealand falcon? Perhaps it was the kea, the cheeky alpine parrot who was forever picking apart the rubber on vehicle windshield wipers in the park. It was a distinction that mattered little, I thought wryly, to the vanished victim.

I knew the Hooker Hut was not far away and looked at my watch: 2:00 P.M. I had been hiking steadily for three hours, so if I turned back now I would arrive at the Hermitage just before dark. However, I knew this was to be a full-moon night, and I hoped to make the hut as a private goal, my own summit. Then again, the clear weather was reportedly due to end, and storms often moved in swiftly and violently.

Suddenly I seemed to have slipped into Antarctica. The temperature dropped to deep freeze. I was in the wind zone I had seen miles down valley. Huge hurricanes of snow were swooping down the slopes, crashing about my ears and slapping across my cheekbones. Ice clung to my face like a strange, blistering growth. Vision was difficult, but as I squinted I could see Mount Cook ahead, and suddenly it struck me I had seen this scene dozens of times before. It looked just like the logo for Paramount Pictures, the first image that appears so often when the theater lights dim. The designer must have been at this very spot, or seen one of Ed's slide shows. But now clouds poured over the pinnacle ridge, and Mount Cook seemed to sway and begin to topple, closing the gap of stark sky over my head. Beneath the howls of the icy wind, I could hear the deep rumbles of the Hooker Glacier. These were perfect windslab avalanche conditions. The fresh, dry blown snow had built up on a hard base on the steep slopes above me, and a layer could release at any time. Still, I felt lucky, and persisted.

The snow was now often waist deep, and it was an effort just to move a few yards. Nonetheless, in the spirit of Hillary, I carried on, stiff (read: frozen) upper lip, using the metal rod markers as short-term goals. But then I fell into a snowdrift and emerged to scan the landscape through the blinding snow. I searched and searched, but in the cold, marble light could find no signs of a marker, no indication of a route upward. I backtracked a few yards and was still lost, and when I scrambled to the top of a boulder where I was barely able to hold on in the gale-force winds, I remained in the dark. What would Ed have done? Continued, no doubt, with little thought. It was like bee-keeping . . . if you dwell on the concept, it becomes too frightening. You just do it.

The elusive hut, which in summertime is really not much of a challenge to reach, being just a walk to the head of the valley where the climbing then gets serious, was still not in sight. No doubt it was just around the alpine spur, an ace and a few minutes away. But I couldn't go on. I was, after all, a manqué mountaineer. Edmund Hillary was something altogether different, part of a historical narrative that is essentially over. He was a figure in the story of heroic adventure that includes Marco Polo, Columbus, Lewis and Clark, Stanley and Livingstone, Peary and Scott, Amundsen, Lindbergh—men with knives in their teeth and ice in their beards—and in their veins. When Ed climbed here he belonged to a time when "because it is there" was a good enough reason to climb a mountain. People are more sophisticated now. Such adventurism seems boyishly foolish at best, environmentally unsound at worst. Man against Nature has taken on a new meaning, I told myself.

I turned back.

Four hours later, *après* glacier, I was in the Hermitage Hotel's luxurious Tavern Bar in front of a blazing fire sipping mulled wine. I had given the barkeep a New Zealand five-dollar note, which featured the face of the country's most famous mountaineer on its frontside. I quietly raised a glass to Ed to celebrate his anniversary.

Doubly happy, however, is the man to whom lofty
    mountaintops are within reach, for the lights
    that shine there illumine all that lies below.

—JOHN MUIR, 1938

THE EIGHTH SUMMIT: MOUNT RAINIER

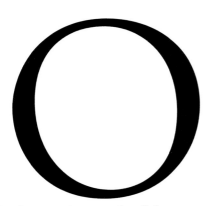O n May 12, 1992, a record thirty-two people stood on the summit of Mount Everest. One was Skip Horner, another his client, Louis Bowen, an American businessman based in Hong Kong. Together they shared a supremely satisfying moment on top of the world. For Skip, forty-four, who had been guiding professionally for twenty years, it was the cap of a long quest...to be the first to guide the seven summits, the highest peak on each of the seven continents.

Six weeks later, at a National Press Club gathering in Washington, DC, Sir Edmund Hillary, conqueror of Everest, gave a talk. In it he recalled the emotions he and Sherpa Tenzing Norgay experienced when they first stood on the crest of Mount Everest on the morning of May 29, 1953. "We felt a satisfaction, and a little humbled, too." But then, in a chiding tone, he commented on the deeds of the previous month: "Everest unfortunately is largely becoming a commercial money-making opportunity. You didn't need to be a schooled mountaineer, not this year. If you were reasonably fit and had $35,000, you could be conducted to the top of the world. How thankful I was that I was active in a pioneering era when we established the route, carried the loads, all worked together for

BORN OF FIRE AND ICE, RAINIER DEMANDS—AND RECEIVES—REVERENCE.

To Native Americans in the Pacific Northwest, Mount Rainier is Tahoma, or "The mountain that was God."

the ultimate objective. The way things are now, I don't think I would have bothered."

Skip Horner had climbed with Sir Edmund's son, Peter, on a Karakoram Peak called Rimo in 1986, and counted him a friend. In March of 1992 Skip finally met the world's most famous mountaineer in Chaunrikarka, Nepal, where he expressed his respect and admiration. Thus, when he heard Ed's lament a few months later, Skip was disheartened. So he wrote to Ed: "I am disturbed by your well-publicized comments disparaging the ascents that were made on Everest this year. Certainly the climb is not now the adventure it was in '53 due to improvements in knowledge and equipment. Still, it takes an extraordinary amount of ability, persistence and luck to reach the top of Everest as the weather and snow and ice conditions are as unpredictable and treacherous as ever...to minimize our achievements does the international climbing community a disservice and does more to minimize the mountain than the climbers...to reach Everest's summit still requires all the physical and mental virtues possessed by you and your mates in '53.... Mr. Hillary, I will always have deep respect for you, but I wonder if you have had the chance to ponder your remarks about us?"

There was no reply.

Somehow Ed's words stirred me as well. It seemed there was a ring to his rave. Hadn't Yosemite, the Grand Canyon, Kilimanjaro, and Victoria Falls all lost some transcendence because of their manufactured and commercial accessibility? When you can hire a guide to do much of the work, doesn't that diminish personal commitment, and thus the quality, the profundity, of the experience? Then again, isn't it elitist to deny others what you have experienced, to preserve in private sanctuary the epiphany that came with a special effort, time, and place? In my years as a river guide I had escorted blind children, senior citizens, and paraplegics down the Colorado River, and I can testify that the transformational aspects of the experience were as vital for them as for the young, hearty do-it-yourself expeditioneers. It may be less of a feat now to climb Everest than in 1953, what with better gear and routes well described, but is the adventure really less, for the guides, for the clients, who feel the same elation and sense of personal achievement on top?

I decided to explore the issue on my own. I had never summited a peak requiring real mountaineering impedimenta: ropes, crampons, nylon slings, carabiners, ice ax, and such. Everest was not in the stars for me. The dormant volcano upon which the first American Everest climbers trained—

THE DORMANT VOLCANO UPON WHICH THE FIRST AMERICAN EVEREST CLIMBERS TRAINED IS A LUSH PARADISE OF VEGETATION AND RUSHING WATER IN ITS LOWER REGIONS.

At 6,400 feet, the area called Sunrise is the highest point in the park reachable by road.

Mount Rainier in Washington—could be. Born of fire and carved by ice, Rainier shoves the rim of its still steaming volcanic crater 14,410 feet into the atmosphere eighty-two miles southeast of Seattle. But, as much as I wanted, I could never attempt such an enterprise on my own. I needed someone to show me how, just as Ed Hillary was first guided when he started climbing on Mount Cook. So I called Skip Horner in Montana. As it turned out, he, too, had never climbed the most heavily glaciated mountain in the conterminous United States. In the spring of 1989 he had made it to the parking lot on the north side, with hopes of a climb up the Liberty Ridge. But the clouds were so heavy, the rain so thick, he never made it out of the car. Skip was ready to try again, and to lead the way.

So it was we gathered at the parking lot in Paradise, 5,400 feet up Rainier's southwest slope, on Saturday, September 11. We were now eight, all friends ready to work together toward an ultimate objective and to carry the loads. With our fifty-pound packs snugly shouldered, we headed up the hill. We stepped lightly through the brooding evergreens, trees that were giants when a British navigator, George Vancouver, sailed the Washington coast in the spring of 1792, presumptuously naming the grand inland peak after a rear admiral in the Royal Navy who had distinguished himself by capturing an

WHEN BATHED IN MORNING LIGHT, IT'S APPARENT WHY MOUNT RAINIER IS ONE OF AMERICA'S MOST POPULAR SIGHTS.

THE PARADISE LODGE—A RETREAT FROM THE BARE ICE AND SNOW OF THE GREAT MOUNTAIN.

WHEN THE WIFE OF THE DEVELOPER OF THE FIRST RESORT HERE FIRST SAW THIS SUBALPINE MEADOW, SHE EXCLAIMED, "THIS MUST BE WHAT PARADISE IS LIKE!" NOW IT IS OFFICIALLY NAMED APPROPRIATELY.

American privateer during the Revolutionary War. The trees gave way to sub-alpine mountain meadows, where several marmots perched trailside were fattening themselves on flowers. A mere fingertip away was the bright volcanic crown, high and lordly as a god. Native Americans of the Pacific Northwest had always known its true name: *Tahoma*, "The mountain that was God."

TWENTY-SIX GLACIERS CLING TO RAINIER, FOREVER CONTRIBUTING TO THE SCORES OF WATERFALLS THAT SPILL FROM THIS GRAND MOUNTAIN.

Now a lenticular cloud bannered across its pinnacle, indicating high winds and the possibility of trouble ahead. I quickly bounded ahead of the pack, and began to think this was not going to be difficult, that my three weeks of running and swimming prior to this venture were paying off. Some eight-thousand climbers attempt Rainier annually, and about 50 percent make at least the crater rim. Yet there is a share of fatalities, more than twenty in the last dozen years. Though I no longer felt the immortality of my twenties, I did feel strong, and confident I would succeed, perhaps even without Skip's help. At Pebble Creek the trail sank into a pocked snowfield, and I continued to plod upwards at a good pace. At a rest stop called by Skip I paused to look around, and felt a chill with the view. The frosty fingers of twenty-six glaciers gripped the cone of Rainier, forming a wonderland of wide snowfields, crevasses, snow bridges, gleaming seracs, and awesome icefalls. This was an unfamiliar world, fantastic and frightening.

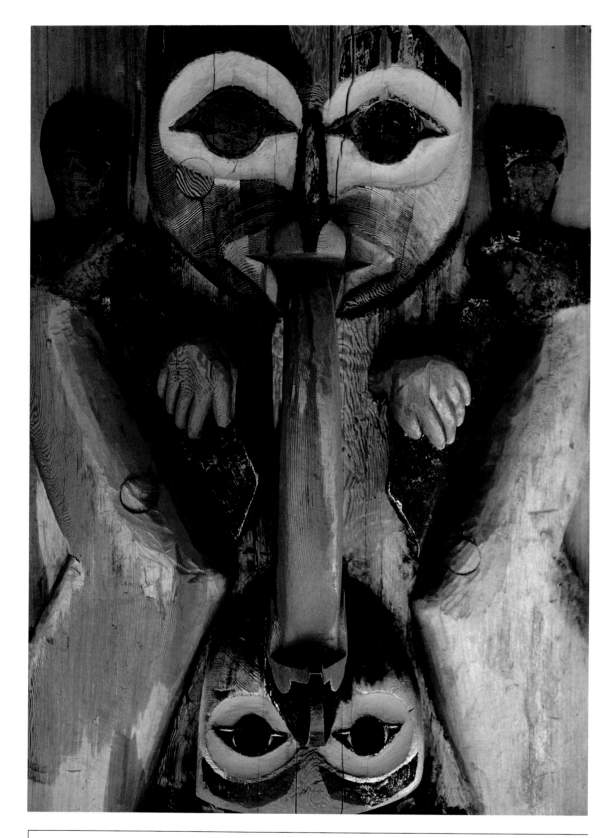

To the region's Native Americans, Mount Rainier represents the sacred and provides wood for the traditional expressions of their beliefs, such as this totem.

When Camp Muir finally came into view, I downshifted, while Skip and three others passed and steamed on up. Maybe I wasn't in such great shape, I reconsidered, as I dragged myself up the pumice-strewn ridge, halfway to heaven at 10,188 feet, and let the pack spill off my back. It was 4:00, six hours after we quit the parking lot. Clouds were boiling up from below, while above the mountain wore a gray-cloud cap. The wind knifed across the ridge, cutting the temperature, and Skip directed me into the low-rock public shelter that squatted in the gap of the ridge between the Nisqually and Cowlitz glaciers.

THE DOUGLAS FIR, WESTERN RED CEDAR, AND WEST-ERN HEMLOCK IN THE LOWLAND FOREST REGIONS OF RAINIER RIVAL THE GRANDEUR OF THE REGION'S COASTAL REDWOODS.

After choosing a wooden bunk, I followed Skip over to the ranger's station, an A-frame hut not much larger than an outhouse, where we met mountain ranger Joe Dreimiller. He told us that of the fifty or so who'd attempted summit climbs that day, none had made it. The winds were simply too high—sixty miles an hour at times, which is enough to blow a man off the mountain. And he warned us about getting onto Disappointment Cleaver. The ice was separating from the rock at the base, and the route was marked by a yellow line the rangers had laid. The ice bridge was on its last legs and would break sometime soon. It was a dangerous crossing.

An hour later I emerged from Joe's hut into a hailstorm to negotiate the two hundred yards back to our shelter. I saw a dim, solitary figure struggling up the embankment. I called down, but got no reply. I called again and he stopped in his tracks. I stepped on down and recognized Howard from our group, who looked dead exhausted, glasses missing from his wan face, sweat gleaming on his scalp like Mylar. I asked if I could help with his pack, and with a nod it was off his back and on mine. Looking at Howard's fallen shoulders and dull eyes I knew then he wasn't going to make it.

With all safely in the hut, Skip whipped up a dinner of Lipton's Parmesan noodles as we recuperated. He announced we would not try for the summit tomorrow. The weather was too bad, the team too tired, and climbing skills were notably lacking. We would spend the following day learning the ropes, so to speak.

All night the wind, like a living thing, sandblasted our shack with ice pellets, and at times it seemed we might be picked up and hurled to California. It would be impossible to climb in this wind, and I began to think of how to deal with the failure of our intended adventure.

But by daybreak the weather had calmed a bit, though the mountaintop remained stubbornly wrapped in clouds. After a lingering

THE CARBON RIVER AREA HAS THE HEAVIEST RAIN-FALL AND MOST LUXURIANT FOREST. SOME BOTANISTS SUGGEST THAT WHAT WE FIND HERE IS A TEMPERATE RAINFOREST, NOT A LOWLAND FOREST.

breakfast, during which I was reminded that water hot enough to boil at two miles high is not very hot at all for a cup of hot chocolate, Skip brought us out onto the glacier for some essential training. Though I had flailed around a bit with some climbing gear while on Mount Blanc some months before, I had never mastered any technique. In fact, I had never really had any lessons. Skip was now an estimable teacher. We learned the crucial techniques of self-arrest, using the ice ax to halt a fall; how to walk "like a cowboy" in the twelve-point crampons so they wouldn't snag on an inseam; and the rules of team survival, including "never step on the rope." By day's end, Howard announced he wasn't going to try for the summit. That left seven.

At 1:00 A.M. Skip woke us up. It was time. The close, stove-fuel air in the shelter was stuffy. We had melted snow the night before, and filled all the water bottles, so it was just a matter of dressing: two layers of Thermax long underwear, Polartec pants and top, a Gore-Tex expedition suit, a parka, inner and outer gloves, two pairs of wool socks, double plastic boots, steel crampons, a harness (the same type used in the opening accident scene in the film *Cliffhanger*, someone pointed out), and a hat. I had brought my Walkman and two books on tape, but Skip said no. This was too dangerous an ascent; one had to be alert to the sounds of falling rocks, to the cries of falling team members. It was an hour before we were on the snow. We roped into two teams. I was second on the string, just behind Skip, a link in a four-man chain. As we waded across the Cowlitz Glacier toward the bare rock bluff of Cathedral Rocks Ridge, I couldn't help but think the rope not only protected against falls, but also prevented runaways. The wind was low, the sky clear.

I had put a set of fresh batteries in my two-inch headlamp the night before, and now I followed the little yellow puddle just ahead of my feet. On our left, the mountain loomed, felt more than seen. Pale snowlight glowed from the empty space below us to the right. The dark mass of the mountain vied with the vacuous space all around, we few fragile climbers caught between the two.

We started up the loose rockfalls of Cathedral Gap, the metal claws of the crampons sparking and scratching against the stone. The path was a dribble of small rocks among the

DESCENDING FROM THE SUMMIT, WE CAN SEE A HANDFUL OF OTHER VOLCANOES IN THE CASCADE RANGE, INCLUDING MT. ADAMS AND OREGON'S MOUNT HOOD.

boulders, and about fifty yards into the debris my left crampon came loose. Embarrassed, I pulled the line, like stopping a bus. Skip turned around, then patiently backtracked to help me reattach the crampon. Then we were off again, clattering up the rocky trail.

Our column of climbers crested the rocky ridge and stepped down onto the ice of the Ingraham Glacier, the frozen river we would follow to the top. We were on the mountain's ice-scoured east face, and the wind seemed to push the darkness up against our backs. The trail was more evident here, a pattern of alternating boot holes in the snow beaten out by climbers in the weeks before us. And then we crossed our first crevasse, a long gash less than a yard wide at the top but cutting hundreds of feet into the ice. Stepping over the black crack, it was easy to envision the tensed 9-mm rope dangling me like bait for the catch.

Not long off the rocks we reached a level stretch known as the Ingraham Flats. Here Skip picked up the pace, but Steve, who was right behind me, was recovering from a bout of flu from just two days earlier and was lagging, so I found myself in a constant tug-of-war between the two.

We walked through the hostile dark another hour, a team in silence, chained souls floating upward together yet alone in our thoughts. Finally, we came to another rocky section…this was the infamous Disappointment Cleaver. We followed the yellow rope across the narrow ice bridge, dimly aware that inches away either side provided a bottomless abyss. Then we were on the Cleaver, another jumble of rotten rock, and we continued up the steep scree. Now my other crampon released, and I scraped the ground for purchase, wrenching my ankle. There had been much in the news lately about how Rainier was going to begin charging climbers for rescues. "Great," I thought, "not only will I fail in this summit attempt, I'll have to pay a small fortune for the privilege." I wished I could divorce my crampons on grounds of metal and physical cruelty and inadequate means of support.

With infinite patience Skip waited as I reattached the crampon in the stinging cold, then stood up. My ankle hurt, but I could still walk, so I signalled thumbs up and Skip's rope went tight. Not too long afterwards, Skip's lamp abruptly died, and Tom, on the rear of our rope, passed his to the front. I was glad I had inserted fresh batteries in my lamp, and mechanically trudged onward behind Skip. But then, not thirty minutes later, my lamp went out. I knew morning light was close at hand, so I volunteered to proceed torchless—not that I had much choice. Now the faint glow from a fingernail moon, the green flashes of the Northern Lights, and the sparks created by my crampons were my only light. I used my hands a lot now while scrambling up.

Finally the darkness dissolved. The mountain looked the same in the pale morning light as it had felt in the pitch of night: angular, distant, coolly impersonal. As the sun approached the horizon, a thick line of neon crimson bled along the edge of the earth. It hung there a long time—it seemed like an hour—before one spot bloomed and the sun rose. In the meantime, distant layers appeared in the rest of the sky, as if glass

plates separated the pink morning air on top from the indigo shadows left from night. Mount Adams, Oregon's Mount Hood, and the open throat of Mount St. Helens in the Tatoosh Range floated like islands in a sea of clouds on the southern horizon.

RAINIER HAS CLAIMED THE LIVES OF AT LEAST SEVENTY-FIVE CLIMBERS SINCE IT WAS FIRST SUMMITED IN 1870. WE HOPE NOT TO ADD TO THAT STATISTIC AS WE CROSS THE HIGH HEM OF THE MOUNTAIN.

Less than an hour after sunrise we reached the upper end of the Cleaver, and stopped for a rest before breaking back into the snow. The wind engulfed us. I was sucking the thin atmosphere deeply, expelling it forcefully. I had no appetite, but drank water greedily. When it came time to bundle up, I couldn't zip my parka, and felt like a helpless child heading onto a winter playground. I asked Skip for help, and like a tolerant proctor, he pulled off his glove and zipped me up. I wanted to give him a hug.

Joe Dreimiller had said it was an easy haul beyond the Cleaver, and I kept reminding myself of those words as I kicked the front points of my crampons into the ice on a near-vertical section. As instructed, we carried our axes in the hand closest to the mountain, the rope in the other, and awkwardly switched one to the other at the elbow of every switchback. Now that it was light, Skip often turned around at these switches to check our progress, and it seemed every time he checked I was tangled in the rope, or worse, stepping on it. I felt like a daft and moonstruck tyro.

Rainier seemed all steep pitches now. We crunched along the glacier's more impressive flotsam. We tramped beneath a skyscraper serac, its sleek sides curving skyward. We jumped the narrow slit openings of crevasses, peering down into the sculptured dark walls that fell away forever. Towering blue ice cliffs curled over us like giant glacial tidal waves, mumbling and groaning as we skirted the edges. Their voices sounded hollow, tubular, and for a moment I felt like I was negotiating the barrel of a very large gun. One such wall collapsed near here in 1981, sweeping eleven climbers into oblivion. Rainier has claimed the lives of at least seventy-five climbers since it was first summited in 1870, and as certain as bad weather will come again there will be more.

Skip had instructed us at the start to keep a coil in one hand, to adjust the slack in the rope between climbers. But as Skip continued, with the pigeon-toed gait of an athlete, he pulled the rope taut between us, and I couldn't maintain a coil. The rope went tight as a banjo string, and I realized Skip was literally pulling me up the mountain. I couldn't keep his pace, and he refused to back off. Exhaustion blanketed my thoughts and limbs, and I began to wonder if I had the endurance to make it. I felt like Howard looked when he reached Camp Muir two days ago. I fought for every breath. I was so bone-deep tired I thought each step might be my last.

"Can we stop for water?" I finally cried, although it seemed to dribble out of my frozen mouth as "Caweesopfoater?" Skip ignored my pleas, or couldn't understand them, and continued to keep the rope taut. I could do nothing but follow. I was too numb to resist. Then, almost without warning, we leveled out at a low wall of brown rock, and Skip dropped his pack. I folded to the ground like a kicked tent and pulled out my last water bottle. The water was frozen. Between breaths I looked around, and saw we were at the brow of a huge crater. On the other side, the western rim, a small, rounded hump rose less than three hundred feet above us. There was nothing beyond. That must be the summit.

So, after perhaps a fifteen-minute break, we re-roped, and began the final walk in the high winds of the near-summit. We crossed the crater caldera, and clambered onto a last staircase of bare rock, steam-cleaned of snow and ice by hissing fumaroles. At 9:40 A.M., we made the last steps to the 14,410-foot-high Columbia Crest, as if kings of the Cascades. Suddenly, the simple act of being present assumed a sense of gathered immediacy. I was overcome with inchoate emotion. I lost control of my face, and submitted to a kind of crazed delight that had me laughing and crying simultaneously. Though thousands, tens of thousands, had stood here before us, I felt this was the first morning on earth, and we the first to bathe in its beauty, unbounded by geography or history. It was a fragment of a cycloramic dream to be on top, and as I hugged the other team members, just as Tenzing Norgay hugged Ed Hillary on Everest, I felt a little humbled, too. I knew I would never have been here without Skip's help, without a thaumaturgic leader who could lift spirits to new heights. In a world shorn of magic, it was the guides who still carried the power. And I knew. There is nothing wrong with guiding people to the upper limits; in fact, there may be nothing more right.

ALMOST NINETY-SEVEN PERCENT OF THE PARK'S 235,612 ACRES WAS DESIGNATED WILDERNESS ON NOVEMBER 16, 1988, PRESERVING THE HABITAT OF AN ABUNDANT ARRAY OF WILDLIFE AND BIRDLIFE.

We Travel not for trafficking alone;
By hotter winds our fiery hearts are fanned:
For lust of knowing what should not be known,
We take the Golden Road to Samarkand.

—JAMES E. FLECKER, 1922

THE TIEN SHAN
MOUNTAINS:
NAVIGATING
UNIVERSAL WATERS

When Soviet Foreign Minister Eduard Shevardnadze and Secretary of State James Baker got together on September 22, 1989, for a superpower arms-control powwow, it wasn't in one of the usual summit locales: Washington, Moscow, Helsinki, Geneva, Malta, or Reykjavik. It was in Wyoming's Grand Teton National Park. And, to break the ice, they didn't play golf, or go sightseeing. They went rafting down the Snake River.

A week later, I pull my raft to shore after a full day of high-spirited white water. After wrapping my bowline around a fat poplar, I flip open my cooler, crack a Löwenbräu, and take a long draw. It is a ritual I'd performed many times before, the moment of physical and mental release after a day of adrenalized adventure. But, today is different. Earlier in the day, before launching, a Kirghizi shepherd had wandered into camp. Sharon Ahern, a publicist for Greenpeace, asked him if he had any environmental concerns. He said he worried about the arms race, and that his valley might be bombed. She asked if he would repeat his statements for the video camera, which would take a few moments to set up.

Later, as we headed into the rapids, I watched with fascination as a homemade cataraft, captained by a grinning young Russian woman, Tanya, plunged into a rapid and its frame snapped. Tanya and her Russian crew paddled the broken

THE CHAKTAL RIVER, TRAVELLING THROUGH THE UNMISTAKABLY REMOTE TIEN SHAN MOUNTAINS.

boat to shore, and soon afterwards the Czechs and the Zambians arrived to help disman- tle the raft. Steve Gilroy, the trip photographer, took advantage of the downtime to ask Misha, our host, about the Aral Sea disaster, which we were scheduled to see in a few days' time.

We are on the Chatkal River, falling from the Tien Shan mountains in Soviet Central Asia. But this is no simple rafting expedition. This is an "eco-adventure"—an adventure with a purpose, a quest for something more than an expensive thrill, a mission to reach higher ground, higher consciousness, and world peace through rafting. Though this effort to wed adventure and global virtue somehow smacks of fashion as we approach the Green Decade, the show was organized by management in my own compa- ny, SOBEK, and I felt compelled to come along and sing the right praises. But the crea- ture we are riding is Hydra-headed—cultural exchanges, citizen diplomacy, world peace talks, environmental investigation, class V rapids. It seems too much to tame on a two- week trip. Nevertheless, here we are.

It wasn't long ago that adventure could stand alone. Mountains were climbed merely to reach summits; wild rivers run for the enticing mix of serenity and physical excitement; journeys were made to reach point B. There was a pureness in the pursuit. Adventure was perhaps a selfish endeavor, one that provided inner rewards, heightened self-esteem, and a feeling of personal achievement, but it did little to help the planet.

Things change. There is a geological shift in adventure. Suddenly ecological and humanitarian causes are au courant. In today's climate of glasnost and global warming, there is a heightened sense that we're all in the same raft, and have to paddle together to get through the century. This is a good and necessary consciousness, but as a former fun junkie I couldn't help but feel that the trend of conspicuously aligning adventure with causes was a thin carapace for vain motives, a marketing technique used to legitimize the hedonism of expeditions, or even a collective cognitive dissonance that said, yeah, we can party in the wilderness because we're saving the planet.

Most expeditions today promote their higher purposes. Will Steger's $11 million trans-Antarctica expedition was "dedicated to increasing world awareness of the magnifi- cent yet fragile seventh continent"; his erstwhile partner, Paul Schurke, led a winter ski and dogsled expedition across the Bering Strait in 1992 to promote Soviet-American friendship and "reconnect the native cultures." The stated objective of Michael Powers' 1990 kayak expedition to Chile was "to promote the formation of national preserves to ensure the protection of irreplaceable endangered features in southern Chile, such as the great Bio Bio River and the Valdivian temperate rainforest that contain the last stand of the giant alerce trees in the world." Promoting world peace is all the rage these days, with peace exchanges taking place within every sport and artistic discipline, even though the cold war seems to be thawing in a microwave.

Project RAFT (Russians and Americans for Teamwork) was the first Soviet- U.S.A. rafting exchange. Started by former SOBEK guides Jib Ellison and Mike Grant in

1987, the original construct was noble and attractive: to take bright young Americans, our future leaders, and put them on a raft with their Soviet counterparts. Together they would paddle the rapids, overcome natural obstacles, and hopefully form a lasting bond that often results from a shared adventure. The raft was a sort of petri dish where positive superpower relations would germinate. Then, thirty years later, when these rafters are in their respective positions of power, it will be that much harder to push the button, knowing friends are on the receiving end. The concept was valid, and Project RAFT enjoyed two years of success, bringing young Americans to Siberia to raft the Katun and other rivers and Soviets to raft the Colorado through the Grand Canyon.

THE SOVIET HOMESPUN "CATARAFTS" THAT ARE MORE NIMBLE AND MANEUVERABLE THAN THE HIGH-TECH AMERICAN VERSIONS. *PHOTO BY RICHARD BANGS.*

SOBEK Expeditions also had permission to conduct adventure tours in the Soviet Union. But in the era of peace exchanges and environmental activism, it was no longer adequate to simply sell adventure. Project RAFT, which was selling seats on its "Citizens Exchange" rafting trips to raise funds for student exchanges, was now a competitor. So SOBEK had to do one better. Thus, the Chatkal River Environmental and Peace Expedition was born, featuring citizen diplomats from not two but four countries.

✛

On the day Shevardnadze and Baker are paddling their Avon inflatable down the Snake, I arrive at Sheremetievo Airport in Moscow, wetsuit and ammo box in hand, ready for eco-action. I deplane with Steve Marks, SOBEK's agent at the ICM talent agency, who is ostensibly on board to evaluate environmental documentary film prospects, but who is really here (I can say with some authority) to have a good time. My pass through immigration is smooth. When the officer notices Steve is from Los Angeles, he points his thumb up and says, "Lakers!" When Steve smiles back, the immigration man sticks his thumb up again and says, "Wayne Gretzky!" Steve nods until his passport is stamped, then shakes his head and says, "Gretzky—NHL hockey, not basketball. Nice try, though."

Meanwhile, I am trying to rent a luggage cart for the eighty pounds of freeze-dried provisions I carried over for the expedition. Only problem is, the cart caretaker only takes roubles. I only have dollars, and the only place to exchange is beyond customs, a classic Soviet catch-22. Just when the situation seems hopeless, a bespectacled, bearded, slightly pot-bellied man wearing a blue SOBEK cap comes crashing through the crowd with a cart, and with a grin stops at my bags and bows deeply. "Michael Harshan, Soviet Travels, at your service," he announces. Within seconds of meeting Michael, or Misha, his real name, we are through customs and sailing through the thick Moscow night in a taxi on the way to the Rossiya Hotel, on the edge of Red Square.

The next morning we meet our comrades in eco-adventure. They include Dominic Mubika, 24, and Alfred Syachelwa, 26, of Zambia, whom SOBEK flew over to be part of this quadrilateral cultural exchange. From Czechoslovakia we have Jaro Lhota, 32, and Martin Hanus, 25, the former a physicist who makes more money washing windows, the latter a sportsman speaking no English or Russian. On the American end we have Chuck O'Bryan, 32, who led the first Western expedition down the Chatkal just three weeks ago; Joe Kaminsky, 32, our videographer; Steve Gilroy, 26, our still photographer; Kirby Ellis, 25, a guide representing Project RAFT; Sharon Ahern, 34, from Greenpeace; Steve Marks, 29, our agent; myself, 39; and Jana Janus, a 49-year-old grandmother from San Francisco, who chucked the capitalist life last year, married a Soviet and moved to Moscow. There are twelve Soviets on the expedition, but only three speak English: Misha, 35, the president of the eighteen-month old Soviet Travels; Vanja Maurakh, 29, a computer programming teacher at Moscow University; and Tanya Sheligina, 27, also a computer specialist, and, like Vanja, a moonlighting river guide for Soviet Travels.

At our get-acquainted breakfast, Chuck hands out red- and blue-colored Chums, the popular cloth straps that secure glasses around fashion-conscious sports lovers' heads, each with the American flag on one side, the Soviet on the other. Even our temples would be constantly reminded of the high nature of this trip.

On the Illyusian-76 night flight to Tashkent, the capital of Uzbekistan, and the Soviet Union's fourth largest city, I see a map of the Chatkal for the first time, and its course becomes clear. Starting in Kirghizia near the China border, it flows west for about eighty miles before reaching the first of scores of impoundments, the Charvak Dam. Later the river merges with the Pskem, and the combined waters are

WITH LESS THAN FOUR INCHES OF RAIN A YEAR, THE LANDSCAPE THAT SUR-ROUNDS THE CHAKTAL RIVER IS PERMANENTLY PARCHED. *PHOTO BY RICHARD BANGS.*

called the Circik, which drains into the Syr-Darya (in ancient times the Jaxartes). The Syr-Darya was once the main feeder river to the Aral Sea, but has been nothing more than a brackish trickle at its mouth for eighteen years. We would be, in a sense, tracing this watercourse from its birth, in the Tien Shan mountains, down to its death at the Aral Sea.

In Tashkent, the command center in Moscow's Afghanistan campaign, we waste no time transferring our eighty-five pieces of gear to two screaming-orange MI-8 21-seater Aeroflot helicopters. Within the hour we are airborne on the ninety-minute flight to the headwaters of the Chatkal, an area known locally as the Golden Cradle. There is a gradual sobering of color as we whop-whop along, into the high desert mountains, and then over the rip in the earth's crust that holds the river itself, a long, shining band of white

THE CHAKTAL WINDS THROUGH THESE MOUNTAINS, WHICH SEEM TO DIVIDE THE PHYSI-
CAL WORLD INTO TWO ARENAS: THE POSSIBLE AND THE IMPOSSIBLE, THE
KNOWN AND THE UNKNOWN, THE IMAGINABLE AND THE UNIMAGINABLE. *PHOTO
BY RICHARD BANGS.*

water. We take turns sticking our heads out the round windows, like dogs in a speeding car, and I look down to a stretch of white water that looks impossible from the air—disconcerting because aerial views tend to flatten perspective, making obstacles, such as rapids, look easier. I grin and shudder at the sight. Class V rapids mean adventure, regardless of trappings; they could also spell trouble, injury, even death in a remote location. This is trouble I've been through before and do not want to repeat.

We land on a gravel bar on a bend in the river, at 4,500 feet, according to the helicopter's altimeter. It takes less than thirty minutes to unload the gear, and with a whoosh the mechanical monsters are gone. All is quiet, save the hushed rippling of the clear Chatkal, and a warm breeze whispering through the poplars and brush willows.

Camp is pitched on a knoll not far from the water, and the afternoon is spent rigging boats. There are three Western-manufactured rafts: a SOTAR, and two Avon professionals shipped from China where they were used on an expedition down the Yangtze I made two years ago. The Western rafts are rigged in a couple hours. The Soviet contraptions, including Misha's kayak, are all handmade from spare parts begged, borrowed, or stolen, and take the rest of the day (and then some) to assemble. Their rafts are essentially crude inflatable catamarans, two large inflated sausages attached with a tinker-toy frame. The pontoon's outer fabric is PVC-coated Dacron, the stuff of truck tarps, and that's exactly where most of the material came from. The crafts look complicated, shoddy, unstable, and flimsy, and the Soviets are proud of their creations, and show them off like new cars.

At dinner, featuring potato gruel and black bread, people begin to wear their badges. Sharon sports her baggy Greenpeace pants; Kirby his Project RAFT sweatshirt; Steve Marks struts with his brand new North Face agent-black fleece Denali Jacket; Alfred, who was born and raised in a grass hut on the banks of the Zambezi, and has never left Zambia before this trip, wears a Drexel Burnham T-shirt, and Misha has a button that says "Joint travel is the best alternative to war" in Russian. I show up with a case of Löwenbräu I purchased at the *Beriozka* (foreign currency) #3 store in Moscow.

A group of sheepherders is camped nearby, and three wander over to visit. They're wearing the traditional Khirgiz Tyrolean-style white felt hats. After some cajoling, they agree to demonstrate their famous horsemanship, and set off galloping through our camp, leaning over and snagging an embroidered cloth full of coins off the ground. The contest is called *Tyiyn Engmei*. Feeling playful, I propose to change the rules a bit. I place a blue SOBEK cap on the ground for one to try, but his horse veers away at the last minute, leery of the unfamiliar fabric, and it takes three tries before the equestrian can snag the prize.

Sharon then asks about their environmental problems, and when they respond with worries about overgrazing and deforestation, lost wildlife and plant life, increasing droughts, and fears of nuclear war, she calls for the videocamera and has them reenact their concerns, sometimes for several takes.

The next morning gives us our first eco-action. The Soviets start to bury the spent Löwenbräu cans, and the Americans leap into action, insisting the cans be crushed and brought back to Tashkent for recycling. "But we don't have recycling," Vanja protests. "If we bring the cans back to Tashkent, they'll just be brought back to the woods someplace and dumped." Still, the Americans argue, that would be a better option than burying the cans along a wild river, where they would tarnish the landscape if they resurfaced. The Soviets counter that if the cans resurface, the shepherds will find and use them, that they wouldn't remain as waste. The Americans think that to be cultural pollution and insist the cans be carted out, so at last they are duly crushed and loaded onto my raft.

After the requisite group photo, we don our river gear and climb aboard our various crafts. The Soviets are a motley bunch, with a hodgepodge of gear. No two pieces look alike. Their lifejackets are hand-sewn affairs, each featuring three plump air bags, two on the chest and one on the back, so that the wearer looks like a well-fed bureaucrat. A worn flap of styrofoam hangs over their fannies, providing protection from the crude frames that jut into their backsides as they kneel and paddle on their catarafts' pontoons. Covering their knees and legs are shin pads, like those worn by Wayne Gretzky. The total effect is an army of retired, ragtag Michelin Men off for a fishing holiday. No candy colors, brand names, trademarks or patents pending here.

Soon thereafter we're on the river, drifting on Soviet waters, something I never really thought could happen. We're among the first fifteen Westerners to boat this river, among the first one hundred to raft in the U.S.S.R. I was born in the antediluvian age of McCarthyism. Schools hammered in the lesson that the U.S.S.R. was a nation of diabolical souls out to destroy us. We practiced squatting under desks, heads tucked in groins, in preparation for the Soviet-launched thermonuclear bomb. Some things didn't change over the next three and a half decades. The last president had called this land The Evil Empire. And now, here I am rafting, giggling along with the Soviets in the next raft, sharing the freedom and giddiness of the wild outdoors. Mark Twain said, "Travel is fatal to prejudice, bigotry and narrow-mindedness." For the moment, my cynicism about all this higher ground stuff drops, and I thoroughly enjoy the moment, being on a river, far from home, but with friends.

The river valley looks like something from the badlands of Nevada: dry, bleached, sparse, snow-capped. It's an area that receives less than four inches of rain a year, about the same as Egypt. We bounce along the blue water over a couple of class I-II rapids, and after barely thirty minutes pull over on the southern bank to explore the Shiite village of Jange-Bazar. Because it is conservative Muslim, Misha instructs us to put on long pants over our shorts before hiking into town.

Two ancient baked-mud mosques sit on a lilac-colored hill overlooking Jange-Bazar, and I begin the climb with Misha. On the way up Misha tells me he has run virtually every wild river in the Soviet Union, and the Chatkal is a favorite. From the sum-

mit we're treated to sensory delights, a spectacular panoramic look at the Tien Shan mountains and the turquoise ribbon of river twisting through it, all with a rock and roll soundtrack, blasting from a P.A. system down in the village. Looking down on the river, we see another Soviet group floating past in catarafts. The Chatkal is indeed a popular

THREE AKTASH RESIDENTS GATHER TO DISCUSS THE DAY'S EVENTS IN THE SUN. *PHOTO BY RICHARD BANGS.*

Soviet run, perhaps the equivalent of our Salmon or Rogue river in the U.S.

Back at the rafts we break for lunch, featuring alphabet soup with Cyrillic letters, watermelon with red seeds and deep red pomegranates (natural coloring for this part of the world), sweet grapes, and warm flatbread, just purchased by Chuck O'Bryan in Jange-Bazar.

Downstream the mountains loom like a great gray tsunami arrested in the act of breaking. A black fissure crooks down the middle, the slot through which the 100-foot-wide river drops. This is the First Gorge, and suddenly we're in it, hemmed in with the water accelerating. Sergey Kirillov, 39, the chief designer of the Soviet gear, is commanding a cataraft with a leaky tube just below his knee, so it seems he may be waterlogged any minute. We in the Western-manufactured rafts make some smug comments about Western superiority in design and function, and wonder if their missiles are as slapped together as everything on this trip.

A few minutes into the dark canyon, Chuck calls for the boats to pull over. We all moor on the right bank, and walk downstream to see what looks like a river of trapped steam spouting from a broken radiator. The torrent, white as bleached bone, pitches over a three-step, thirty-five-foot fall that is impossible to run. So we begin the long, tedious process of disassembling our high-tech rafts and carrying heavy frames, oars, and rafts themselves over the boulders down to a quiet spot at the base of the rapid. This exercise takes gruelling hours. Not for the Soviets, however. They simply pick up their ultra-lightweight, homemade, low-tech catarafts, balance them above their heads, and walk to the waterfall's end. In fifteen minutes the Soviets are through with their task and back to help us move our rafts.

"Odin, dva, tri"

"Komodzi, kawali, katatu"

"Jedna, dva, tri"

"One, two, three"

Countrymen from each of the four nations help hoist the rafts, and each takes a turn counting as we heave the rafts on cue. If the Soviets are smug in the knowledge that their rafts outperformed the expensive Western models in the first test, they don't show it. Instead they join us in a spirited chorus of "Song of the Volga Boatmen" as we continue the portage.

That night the group comes together for the first time, and the tapestry of our common humanity is spread over our little camp. Wheat Vodka is the shuttle that weaves this tapestry. Sergey announces he's a "party dog" and produces the quart-sized, 192-proof spirit that also serves as a firestarter in rainy weather. "May the troubles in your house be as few as the drops in your glass," Misha toasts, and we all slam back our shots. Before long we're singing "Hey, ho, nobody home," in rounds, in both English and Russian. All four nationalities tell bad jokes in turn, and each tries to outdo the next. The winner, a variation of an old standard snipe at the system, comes from Jana: "A Russian finally gets enough money to buy a raft. He goes to Sergey and picks it out. Asks when it will be delivered. 'Ten years,' Sergey says. 'Will that be the morning or afternoon, because the plumber is coming in the morning?" Jaro pulls out his harmonica, I pull out mine, and we do a dueling banjos routine on mouth harps. It reminds me of the scene in *Casablanca* when the French and Germans in Rick's Café engage in a battle of their national anthems, only here it's truly in good spirits.

The next morning's float is quiet and brief. We soon pull over to explore the last village en route, Aktash, a sheep-and-farming collective of about a thousand people. Walking into Aktash is like walking into Genghis Khan's encampment. The faces are round, the eyes oblique, frames short and narrow—the Asiatic features of nearby southern Siberia and Mongolia. In fact, the Aktashians are descended from the Turco-Mongol hordes that invaded the area in the thirteenth century. Czarist Russia effortlessly annexed the region in the late nineteenth century, the fur hats conquering the skullcaps.

Resentment against the hegemony, against atheists, against communists, still runs deep, but for us it is a friendly place. Within minutes of arriving we are ushered into the dim room of a young couple, Cherkesh, 31, and Tamara, 21, both Aktash teachers and new parents. They have us sit on the floor around a long table for a snack. Tamara quickly serves us a beggar's banquet of local delights: bread, apples, dried apricots, hard candy, watermelon, raisins, and green tea poured in half-cup servings, so that we will stay and have more, or so we are told.

After some excellent food and cheer, Tamara asks Jana to hold her baby, named after 'gold' in Russian. She takes out a three-stringed instrument called a *homus*, and starts to play and sing love songs. Her voice is high and tremulous, and her notes sail over the room like a small boat in a light wind. The moment is beautiful, a concert as pure as innocence. Tamara tilts back her head, wrapped in a traditional cotton scarf, closes her eyes, and reaches new notes as her fingers fly across the homus. We cannot understand a word, but she reaches us, and reminds us that we all share the same desires and emotions. As we stand to leave I stare at a colorful map on the wall showing the course of the Chatkal. Cherkesh, noticing my fascination, suddenly untacks the map, and presents it to me. I reach for my wallet, but he shakes his head vigorously and smiles. I have nothing to give him in return, or so I think until I check my pocket. There I find my old Hohner harmonica, which I press into his hand while bidding goodbye.

That night, to break the monotony of the Soviet menu, I pull out a no. 10 can of freeze-dried peas, and bring it to the table as a peas offering. Vanja reciprocates by producing not-so-fresh sheep liver, a gift from shepherds we passed yesterday. It is a big hit for the Soviets, but not the Americans, so to salvage the evening I produce marshmallows and Jiffypop, treasured items for our comrades, junk food for us, but food that tastes like a million roubles at the moment.

After dinner Misha lights up several five-inch slabs of Plexiglas, which he uses as candles, and tells me there are no members of the Communist Party on this trip, not even Sergey the party dog. He goes on to explain a piece of his rafting partners' philosophy, that in the Soviet Union a person can be only two of three things: clever, honest, and a member of the Communist Party. If one is a member of the party and honest, then he is not clever; if he is a member and clever, then he's not honest. And, of course, if he is like the Soviets on our trip, he is clever and honest, but cannot possibly be a member of the Communist Party.

The next day, Thursday in some parts of the world, we slide into the scenic third gorge of the Chatkal. Serrated peaks loom in the distance like the ramparts of a forbidden city. *Copokas* (magpies), black with white-tipped wings, flitter between juniper trees on the banks, and the unfeeling walls arch higher, turning the room into an amphitheater. Kirby takes out his Walkman and speakers, puts on Talking Heads' "Take me to the River," and we rock and roll down the river. At lunch Kirby finds bear tracks along the beach, and Vanja points upwards as a bald eagle soars with the canyon updrafts.

The day brings the first runable rapids of size, Jil-Chekam and Niza, and some new vegetation: cherry and apple trees. At a smoke stop, near a yurt fashioned from animal skin, I ask Vanja, a certified white water instructor, about Soviet rafting. He says the Soviets have been boating white water since the late thirties, when loggers and climbers used foldboats to carry them into remote wilderness regions. It was about the same time white water rafting was becoming a sport in America, though neither nation knew the other was discovering the same thrills and spills.

The evolution continued in a somewhat parallel way. In the sixties the Soviet rafters started using discarded Aeroflot survival rafts as their vehicles for wild river navigation, and, coincidentally, I started rafting in the Appalachian mountains the same time using an old Pan Am model. Then in the seventies the parallels began to bend. Because many of the better wild rivers in the U.S.S.R. had no road access and all gear had to be carried in, the resourceful began to handmake lightweight catarafts, which could literally be backpacked anywhere and were quicker and nimbler on the water than the survival rafts. The new designs became popular, then standard, and now Soviet river runners swear the best of the West just doesn't compare. Soviet river running also differs in that there are no commercial operators, who dominate stateside rafting. Instead there are scores of rafting clubs throughout the country, and in free time members take off and run rivers. There are thirty clubs in Moscow alone. And, as if to make Vanja's point, three Soviet rafting groups float by while we're sitting on the river's edge.

Next stop is Arab Rapid, named for an abandoned village on the left bank, a village conquered by the Prince of Destruction himself, Tamerlane, in 1396. It was here two weeks ago that Chuck O'Bryan, prince of the river, almost met his own destruction. The Soviet homespun boats had run the class V rapid first without mishap, but when Chuck made the attempt, he crashed into a reversing wave, which stopped his raft, surfed it over to an enormous hole, and flipped it over as though it were a rubber duck. The icy water took the wind out of Chuck and his three passengers, but no one suffered injuries—at least physical ones. The pride in superior American technology, know-how, and skills seemed as fragile as the broken oar Chuck fished from the river.

Arab Rapid proves no problem for any of the various boats or countrymen on this trip. Chuck recruits the two Zambians to paddle the front of his raft, and they do so with such vigor they're nicknamed the Evinrudes, after the outboard motors, and the tiny American flag Chuck flies at the stern snaps as though on a speedboat. Chuck's raft motors past the hole that capsized the same raft less than a month ago.

The next two days are to be layovers, a chance to hike the countryside, hunt for walnuts and apricots, and perhaps explore the next valley north, the Koksuu watershed. But the night brings heavy rains, the morning hills are dusted with new snow (the first the Zambians have ever seen), and the weather is cloudy and cold. Few are thrilled with the prospect of a long hike on such a blustery day. So we set up a volleyball net and dedicate the day to games, including rousing sets of Yahtzee, Hearts, Hollywood Rummy,

THE FALLS MIRROR THE PURE BEAUTY AND UNRESTRAINED POWER OF THE MOUNTAINS THAT TOWER ABOVE. *PHOTO BY RICHARD BANGS*.

and the Soviet Union's most popular card game, Preference, a cross between Bridge and Euchre. It's also a chance to get to know our comrades on this expedition. Misha reveals he has a Ph.D. in biochemistry, but gave up all claims to science to be a river runner and president of his little enterprise, Soviet Travels for Peace and the Environment under the Soviet Peace Committee, our official host organization for this eco-adventure. Misha explains that in the Soviet Union the length of an organization's name is directly related to its clout. "More words, more power," he grins, and then suggests if we want real respect in the Soviet Union we should change the name from SOBEK Expeditions to "SOBEK's International Organization for Global Exploration, Expeditions and Worldwide Adventure Travel."

On the second afternoon of the layover, Sergey builds a *banya*, a riverside sauna, by constructing an A-frame from acacia branches covered with plastic tarps. Just outside the tent, he builds a bonfire, into which he pours dozens of softball-sized rocks. When the rocks are red-hot, he shovels a load into the tent and calls all the men over to his creation. Stark naked, we crowd into the dark, sweaty room, pour water onto the glowing rocks, and, as the steam rises, swat one another with willow branches. Then, when we can't take it any longer, we run out and dive into the glacial-melt Chatkal. Nothing has ever been as exhilarating, and after each of us repeats the ceremony a few times, we head back to camp, and the women give it a try.

Just as the sun sets, we all reassemble around the kitchen table, and I bring out a half-gallon bottle of Stolichnaya. We trade risque toasts, and a few minutes later the bottle of Stoli is empty. The Zambians entertain the group by singing a jazzy a cappella tribal song in their native tongue (Nyanja), with Dominic on percussion employing an overturned Igloo cooler as his drum. The crowd loves the Zambians' music, breaks into dance, and has them repeat the chorus over and over, as the party gets rowdier and rowdier. We're suddenly all party members, the Pantagruelic Party.

The next day, Sunday, we're back on the Chatkal, which now moves like spilled paint with the added rainwater and silt. Just a mile downstream two men wave my raft over at a honey farm. I oblige, and Steve, Sharon, and I bound over to meet more river people. The older man, wearing a gold silk-embroidered skullcap, invites Sharon to sit on his horse, which she does with glee as I snap photos. Then the younger man, a teenager, helps Sharon off, and gestures that he wants a photo with her. I raise my Maxxum and look through the viewfinder. Suddenly, I blink with disbelief as the man grabs Sharon and tries to kiss her. Sharon's smile turns to a panicked frown, and she tries to push the man away. He persists, pulling her closer in a tight grip, and plants his mouth on her cheek. Sharon squawks, struggles free, and briskly makes her way to the raft, as the two men stare lustily. It is an ugly scene, and stains the innocence of our trip, changing the way any of us will approach strangers.

Soon, though, we are barreling through rapids, sharing the sunshine and scenery with our proven friends. Then, in a medium-sized rapid, Tanya's cataraft falls over a rock, and the aluminum frame snaps in two. The boat limps to shore, where it is disassembled, and its pieces distributed among the other rafts. Tanya and her crew likewise crowd onto the remaining boats, and then hang on as the packed flotilla navigates the rapids for another couple miles. We're all warned to be certain to pull over above Harkush, the worst rapid on the Chatkal.

It is near impossible to miss the marker at the entrance to Harkush: a six-foot-high stone monument with crossed paddles perched atop the right bank. It is a memorial to Nina, a twenty-five-year-old woman who attempted the run with friends in 1975. The boat capsized, and she drowned. Now, a black-and-white photo of a beautiful dark-haired young woman looks out over the rapid to warn of the potential consequences of attempting Harkush. Following tradition, we lay fresh flowers in front of Nina's stare before looking at the rapid.

We spend hours scouting the mile-long rapid, a roaring, misting diadem of plunging water. We mentally trace possible routes, but each ends with a death-defying move, a high-risk maneuver that could cause severe injury to boats or persons. Once one piece of the puzzle is solved, one section of the rapid mentally mapped, another preposterous riddle presents itself. Trying to choose a route through this maelstrom is a bit like grappling with a Russian *matrushka,* a carved wooden peasant doll that opens to reveal yet another carved wooden doll, and another, and so on.

By the time we've surrendered, the Soviets have already portaged their catarafts and are busy hewing birch branches to replace the broken frame. Kirby and I decide to maneuver our rafts down the first few hundred yards of the rapid and pull over at the brink of the fireworks to shorten the dreaded portage. Kirby goes first, with Jana helping to paddle the bow, and executes a perfect run. I wait for Steve Marks and Sharon to show and help paddle my boat, but after ten minutes, I'm impatient, and when Misha walks into view, I invite him to join me. He grins devilishly, dons his hockey helmet, and leaps into the bow of my raft.

I pull away from the shore, and point into the maw of Harkush, Misha leaning over the bow like a gargoyle. Then, as the current grips the raft, I begin to pull on the oars, and move us to the right...but we don't move. Something's wrong. Misha is paddling the opposite direction like a madman. I yell at him, but the roar of the rapid drowns me out. I correct, and begin to row in the direction Misha is paddling, but he switches and paddles the opposite way again. I have no control over the raft, as it drops into the rapid, toward the worst section, the section where Nina drowned. I try to yell louder, but get no response, so I instead try to overpower Misha's strokes with my own, and pull like another madman toward the shore. Just at the threshold of the worst section, I wrestle the boat to shore. And Misha turns and smiles his rascally grin.

With the fair-skinned light of dawn I poke my head out of the tent to see what has become the usual first sight: our Russian hosts scurrying around the kitchen, washing dishes, brewing coffee, busily preparing another mushy bland meal for the international group. *"Dobray ootra* (Good morning)!" Vanja calls out with a smile. None of the Americans is even out of bed yet. Although the no-incentive communist system is supposed to create lazy workers, I have never seen people work harder than the Russians on this trip. They are not relics of a clogged, oppressive culture. At every juncture the Russians out-sweat, out-perform the otiose capitalists, and are forever looking out for the interests of others. I mention this to Jana, who says this is one of the pluses of socialism. There was never a Me Decade in the Soviet Union; people learn to live and work for the group, and genuinely put others' wants and needs ahead of their own. In the microcosmic universe of a wild river canyon, socialism looks pretty good, and I'm inspired to hurry into the kitchen to see if I can help.

Soon after a cornmeal mush breakfast we're back on the river, and the rapids continue in spades. The mackerel-skyed morning is spent running a long piece called Kishlaksay, and then we pull over to scout a continuous two-mile stretch called Pegak. The rapid is so long and complex that Kirby jokes I should draw a map of the intended route and tape it to the bow. Not a bad idea, and with the route fresh in my mind, I etch it out on a piece of notebook paper and tape it to the bow facing me.

The second wave to wash across the bow snags my map, yet the run is still good, and in the eddy below we pull over for a breather and lunch: blini and gruel for the Soviets, Chuck's private stash of Skippy's chunky peanut butter and Hershey's chocolate for the Americans. Then back to the river for a pyrotechnic finale of rapids. For hours the rapids just keep coming, all runable, all exciting, all wet. It is the best single afternoon of rafting I've ever encountered. It's as though an architect designed the ultimate four-hour raft ride.

By the time we reach the fifth and final canyon we are giddy. At the last gate, a spot where the river chokes to barely a raft's width, Chuck, Kirby, and I crash into one another, causing a three-raft pile-up that has us spinning and laughing in the currents before each is flushed through. In minutes the canyon tapers, the water slackens, and a hush falls over the group. The river makes its final adjustments, like a settling stomach. We're at the end of the run, at the beginning of the Charvak Reservoir, the first of hundreds of man-made impoundments on the Aral Sea feeders. A haunting wind blows that night, making it impossible for most to sleep. The winds of change, someone comments over porridge at breakfast.

We wait for the bus to pick us up at the Charvak Bridge, and listen attentively as a local environmental scientist, Professor Valery Danilov of the Uzbek Academy of Sciences, tells us about how a reserve has been set aside to help save the wildlife of the region. Professor Danilov discusses the problems with the twenty-year-old dam: its diversion of water from the Aral, its potential for crumbling if an earthquake strikes in this seismically active area, its effects on the local ecology.

When the bus departs for the 120-mile trip to Tashkent, Vanja takes the microphone and elaborates on the environmental issues as the evidence passes outside the windows. His English is difficult to understand over the tinny loudspeaker, and the subject, though I know it is important, is not stimulating. We've just completed a thrilling adventure, one that stood well on its own merits as a pure endeavor, and once again we were trying to elevate it all with significance. I turn off Vanja's voice in my mind and fall asleep.

The vodka flows freely throughout dinner that night at the Tashkent Hotel. By the second course of *pyelmeni* (meat dumplings), we're all toasting each other, bathing in the success of our river journey. We discuss the goals achieved so far: international cooperation and understanding; discovery of new compassions for our fellow man; recognition of basic human equality. In the midst of all these drunken self-congratulations I notice the Zambians off in a corner quietly drinking by themselves. "That's not right," I complain to Jana, who is sitting across from me. Immediately she gets up and goes to speak to Dominic. I watch as she cajoles and gestures, and then the Zambians break out into their song, pounding the table in rhythm. It captures the attention of the rest of the group, and soon everyone has crowded around the Zambians, and is clapping time to the African beat. It's a few raucous, fun minutes, but something about the show bothers me, and though I clap and smile, I never leave my seat. Then a wave of misanthropy washes over me.

THE HIGH DESERT MOUNTAINS THAT ARE CALLED THE TIEN SHAN OR THE "MOUNTAINS OF HEAVEN." THE CHINESE BELIEVE THESE MOUNTAINS ARE A HEAVENLY ABODE FOR TAOIST IMMORTALS. *PHOTO BY RICHARD BANGS.*

After several flashy choruses, the Zambians bow and retire to their room. Jana returns to her seat across from me, beaming a beatific smile. "Isn't it amazing what we're doing? We're really changing the world. With all these exchanges, we're making adventure meaningful," she says.

"I'm not so sure," I counter. "I understand the U.S.-Soviet exchange, and even the Czechs seem to fit into the scheme. But Zambians? Isn't this round-peg-in-square-hole stuff? Why are the Zambians here? To further relations between our countries? No. Zambia is a nonaligned nation. The Zambians are here as part of a gimmick, a contrivance to justify our fun, an excuse to give added meaning to our adventure. In fact, I think it's worse than that. I think our bringing the Zambians here is racist in the Cotton Club sense. They're here for our entertainment. The only time we pay attention to the

Hanging in the heart of the Tien Shan Mountains is the Shiite village of Jange-Bazar, where a farmer heads down toward the river to check his crops. *Photo by Richard Bangs.*

Zambians is when they sing for us. If this were a rafting exchange between white supremists in South Africa and black Zambians, then the effort could be understood, applauded, championed. It might do some good. But shipping Zambians to the Soviet Union to raft with Americans and Russians is an excuse to make us look good, and it smacks of opportunism. And that goes for the Aral Sea as well. Tomorrow we're off to see the environmental problems of the Aral. Why are we doing this? We're not scientists. We had a great time running the Chatkal. Can't it stand at that? Why do we have to tack on relevance? Why muddy the joy with meaning? What happened to the purity of adventure?"

Jana is appalled. "You're crazy. You're missing the point. There can be as much joy in learning as in self-indulgent adventure. We're just wedding the two, and it's time. I learned a lot having the Zambians on board, and yeah, they entertained me, but we entertained them. And we're all better for it. As for the environmental aspects of this trip, it makes me feel good, better than the thrill of running a rapid, to know I'm working towards saving the planet between having fun. If you can't see that, you're blind." Jana, the grandmother, a former drug addict turned successful businesswoman, slams down her vodka glass and stalks off to bed.

The next morning Misha walks into the breakfast room with a stranger, a member of the Communist Party from Moscow sent to join us. Misha tells us the Aral Sea excursion could be cancelled, that final permission might be denied by central government authorities. I'm secretly relieved, but before the last cup of coffee is downed, Misha returns from a phone call with the news that the planes are ready.

At the airport we walk across the tarmac to two 1949 An-2 propeller biplanes, looking like something out of *Lost Horizon*. "God's Speed," my pilot says in accented English as he starts the engines, and soon we're hurtling northward over the Hungry Steppes to the terminus of the Chatkal waters, the Aral Sea.

After crossing the invisible border into the Karakalpak Autonomous Republic (a subdivision of Uzbekistan, named for the indigenous Turkic ethnic minority) we land at its capital, Nukus, on the shores of the waterless Amu-Darya River (the Oxus of ancient times). It is a brief stop for refueling and a meeting with elegiac local officials who tell us we're just the second group of Americans to visit the Aral Sea in over thirty years. The first was led by *National Geographic* editor Bill Ellis just three weeks ago. All others who tried over the years were turned away.

Suddenly we all feel privileged. And as the propellers rev for the final takeoff, the cabin is uncharacteristically somber. We fly over the edge of the Kyzyl Kum Desert, one of the bleakest in the world. It is a brutal landscape, one that gets drier and more barren with each mile. Nonetheless, all eyes are glued to the windows. There is a sense we are witnessing something special.

As we approach the Aral we began to see what looks like toy ships listing in the desert. They appear to be perfect miniatures, Tonka toys dropped from the sky into a sandbox. No water is in sight. Misha says there used to be so many lakes here, from the air it looked like Finland. Minutes later we see the Aral itself, a blue oasis rimmed by residual white salt and sand. We land at Muynak, 225 feet above sea level, once a thriving port town, now landlocked forty-five miles from the Aral, and dying. In 1960 there were thirty-one thousand people in Muynak; today just twenty thousand. A fish processing plant and cannery is its only means of employment, yet there are virtually no carp or sturgeon left in the Aral. So the government flies in frozen fish from the Baltic Sea, 1,700 miles away, to keep the citizens of Muynak employed.

With the mayor of Muynak as our tour guide, we pile into an old bus and chug into the desert toward a perished resort, getting stuck in the fine grains of salt and sand along the way. There are no trees or bushes to which we can attach a winch cable, so we all file out and push. More than ten thousand square miles of newly exposed sea bottom are so encrusted with salts from the lake that almost nothing grows.

Finally we reach our destination, the ship cemetery we'd seen from the air. The sight up close is awesome; it takes my breath away. Dozens of huge iron fishing trawlers and other boats are tipped and partially buried, as though tossed miles inland by a massive tidal wave. But that wasn't the story at all, as the mayor explains and Misha translates: "In the winter of 1974 the sea withdrew quickly, and by spring, when the boats were usually launched, they were high and dry, and it was impossible to move them."

As we wander among the twisted steel and rusted bellies and the anchors in the sand, it is a ghastly sight. It is hard to believe this has happened in the late twentieth century.

Back in Muynak we're ushered into a conference room and served salty tea as the local officials begin to speak to us about the Aral Sea. The conference begins with a bang as one man with a furrowed face announces that the Aral Sea disaster is "ten times worse than Chernobyl."

This wakes us up, and the room becomes a charged center of angry discussion and accusations. In the calm moments I learn from Tanya, who translates, that the Aral was once the fourth-largest freshwater lake in the world (after the Caspian, Lake Superior, and Lake Victoria), but it has shrunk to a shadow of its former glory. It now ranks sixth. To date it has lost 66 percent of its water, 95 percent of its fish, and in its wake a salt and dust Sahara lays, a fallow graveyard and monument to resource mismanagement. If nothing is done, experts predict the Aral will dry up completely by the year 2000.

"What caused all this?" I ask incredulously.

Tanya explains in an inky accent that naturally underlines words. In the post-Stalin rush toward industrialization there were hasty decrees to increase the gross cotton output of Uzbekistan and the Karakalpak Autonomous Republic. Officials sanctioned scores of man-made diversion projects on the Aral's two sources, the Syr-Darya (into which the Chatkal flows) and the Amu-Darya. Water was siphoned from the two watersheds in an effort to irrigate new lands and produce higher cotton yields, as mandated by the central government. The diversion projects were so grossly inefficient and exces-

THE SHIP CEMETERY AT THE ARAL SEA; NOW A PERMANENT EXAMPLE OF RESOURCE MISMANAGEMENT. *PHOTO BY RICHARD BANGS*.

sive in their thirst, the lower reaches of the two rivers were reduced to little more than sewers and today virtually no fresh water reaches the Aral.

"What will happen if the Aral completely dries up?" I ask, now completely absorbed with the issue.

Tanya postulates that consequences are both local and global in scope; ecological, economic, and social in range. Already the climate has been altered; there is less rain, average temperatures have risen, and the growing season has appreciably shortened. The result is a dramatic decrease in cotton and other crop yields. As the sea has shrunk it has become increasingly saline (44 percent salt in some places), killing its native fish population. To survive, locals have had to turn to more land crops, yet the area, already the driest in the U.S.S.R., has become more parched. To compensate, local farmers have turned to toxic herbicides and fertilizers. These poisons have leached into the water table around population centers, and now the Aral region shows soaring rates of hepatitis, intestinal infections, jaundice, typhoid, and cancer. It has the highest infant mortality rate in the country (eighty deaths per one thousand births). At one time 173 animal species lived around the Aral, including tigers. At last count just thirty-eight remained.

The newly formed Aral desert has created enormous dust and salt storms that have damaged crops hundreds of miles away. Some estimate that 5 pecent of the particle dust matter circling the earth's inner atmosphere comes from the Aral area, contributing significantly to the greenhouse effect. Salt rains have dropped Aral salt as far west as the Black Sea coast, and as far north as the Soviet arctic shore. And, as the Aral recedes the frequency and magnitude of its storms grows. The salt, as it spreads, not only kills cash crops, but trees, wildlife, and vital pastureland used for livestock.

"What's the solution?" I ask, bewildered by a crisis I never knew existed.

Many believe it's too late, that nothing can be done, Tanya answers. Others argue for a grand diversion canal from a Siberian river, the specter of astronomical cost and unknown ecological effects notwithstanding. Still others believe hope lies with the international community, that as yet unconceived solutions will be devised only if enough people around the world become aware and concerned with the catastrophe.

With that I raise my hand to speak to the room of Muynak citizens. "Why did you invite us here? Why not invite *The New York Times*, the BBC, CBS, or some major media? When the Chernobyl accident was publicized in the international press, help was on its way within hours; same with the Armenian earthquake. Why invite us, a group of adventurers?"

A wrinkled man in ragged clothes stands and answers me.

"Because you are the only ones the central government has allowed to visit us. They believe you are harmless because you are tourists. The important international media have been denied. We are Muslim, and the government is anti-Islam. The Kremlin is committing cultural genocide with the Aral catastrophe. They don't want the world to know. We do. This disaster has been contained for thirty years. It is a crime of silence.

You received permission to visit us precisely because you are a tour group, which poses little threat to the Moscow bureaucrats. But now we ask you to help us. If you can tell the world of this disaster you could help save our lives, and the lives of our children. You must help us."

I look back and forth at the various members of our expedition exchanging stunned looks. The idea had been to sprinkle our adventure with a little pertinence, not to glaze it with guilt, to recruit some compassion for the issues, not join the army. Suddenly, though, I feel like enlisting. I stand up.

"We will help. We will tell everyone we know of your situation, of the Aral Sea, of the problems that affect you and all of us. We will help to seek a solution." As I sit down, the room is silent. I lock eyes with Dominic, whose huge smile overwhelms his face. He begins to clap. Steve Gilroy is snapping photos; Joe Kaminsky is running his video recorder; Jana is nodding. When the translation finishes there is scattered, cautious applause among the Muynakians. They've heard many promises many times before, but hope still waters their eyes. Chuck then stands and begins to tell of how he grew up in southern Arizona, and when his community faced a similar problem, cotton growing was cut back, and more efficient irrigation and growing methods were initiated. Chuck continues in his measured delivery, and I drift off again, looking out the window at a landscape as desolate as the maria of the moon.

I think to myself that I really have been affected by what I've seen and heard, and that Jana was right. At that moment, possessed of a passion to help, I felt more energized than I had at any time running the river. The adventure had been great, spirits had sparked, emotions soared. But now there was a higher high. Jana was right about the Zambians, about the environmental tie-ins. The important part was connecting, engaging, comprehending the problems, and feeling like a part of the solutions. Adventure travel can do that. We just had. And I wondered if I could ever just run a river again, or if I would ever want to.

And on that day Eduard Shevardnadze returned to the Kremlin with his reports, analyses, insights, and agenda, and things actually began to change.

*S*he Who Is Filled With Food

—THE ENGLISH TRANSLATION OF "ANNAPURNA"

ANNAPURNA:

A ROOM WITHOUT A VIEW

I f there is a woman's mountain, it must be Annapurna, the consort of Shiva, and the goddess of abundance. And as men are drawn to women, I was drawn to Annapurna.

Alone in a North Face tent, still half owned by sleep, I hear the low, distant sound of the mountain chanting. As consciousness comes, the sound seeps closer, then fades into the round depth of a Buddhist descant...it is Ngati Sherpa, in the canvas tent next door, saying his morning prayers.

As the black vulture flies, I am less than a mile from its gate, the entrance to the Annapurna Sanctuary, the four- by two-mile egg-shaped alpine basin surrounded by nine icy summits higher than 21,000 feet. It should be an easy matter to penetrate this portal, but the air vibrates with uncertainty. By no design, I am travelling with a female contingent: four women clients, our thirty-three-year-old leader Maureen Decoursey, and Archie, who is so quiet and passive he seems gelded. And yet one woman is missing...

We're on the seventh day of our trek up into the Annapurna Himal. In 1978, the throne room of the mountain goddess Annapurna was the objective of the first American Women's expedition to an 8,000-meter peak. On October 15, after a long and perilous climb, Vera Komarkova and Irene Miller succeeded in reaching the sum-

THE MOUNTAIN GODDESS ANNAPURNA AT 23,607 FEET. NOTHING GROWS UP HERE, BUT THE SPARKLING PEAKS LOOK ALIVE.

IT SEEMS AS IF WE TRAVEL THROUGH A WORLD OF CHILDREN—NEPALESE CHILDREN ARE EVERYWHERE—AS WE WIND UP THE TRAIL INTO THE ANNAPURNA SANCTUARY.

mit. Tragically, two members of the expedition, Alison Chadwick-Onyszkiewicx and Vera Watson, disappeared on the mountain two days later, and their bodies now lie enshrined in the soft snows up ahead. We are stepping up a slippery trail that rises six thousand feet in five miles, alongside white water and between walls never more than a half mile apart or less than three thousand feet high. The weather has been unseasonable and unreasonable. It's been raining for days, and we've resorted to looking at postcards to catch the grandstand views supposedly outside our tent doors. Now that we've reached a higher altitude, it's snowing. For the last several hours we've passed a river of trekkers retreating down the trail, shaking heads and warning in a dozen accents that avalanches ahead make it impossible to continue.

Now, at Hinku Cave, as we stop for thrice-brewed milk tea and hard-boiled eggs, Maureen looks worried. She is hunched in solemn conversation with Ngati, our sirdar and veteran of three Everest Expeditions, including one with legendary British mountaineer Chris Bonnington. His flat, Apache-like face is leathery and lined from years in the mountains, and it now telegraphs intensity. Finally, Maureen turns to us and announces the plan. Despite the fact that the clients had travelled halfway around the world, and paid $2,500 each, plus air fare, to be guided up into the Annapurna Sanctuary, the dangers are too high. The heavy snow has created high-risk avalanche conditions in the final, narrow entrance to the sanctuary. In fact, a half dozen major avalanches have already spilled into the gorge, and the lodge owners at the Machapuchare Base Camp have evacuated.

There is a communal sigh with the news. Theresa Blackburn had scheduled this trip so she could celebrate her fiftieth birthday within the embrace of the Annapurna Sanctuary. Everyone wants to reach the goal of this journey—and I'm no exception. I have been the sturdiest hiker, and have my private reasons for wanting to reach the inner sanctum. Maureen must sense my compulsion to continue, because just as my heart is sinking with the news, she turns her gaze on me and says, "I will allow one exception: Richard, who is the strongest, fastest hiker, can continue with the help of Ngati and Dawa Lama. The rest of us will turn back and camp at the Himalaya Hotel." At that moment I wonder if Maureen, who has been studying Buddhism for years, is a *dakini*, one of the female deities who guides mortals to wisdom. She is sending me up the path.

Perhaps I should be noble and say, "Thanks, but no thanks, I'll stay with the group." But I can't. I know I have to try to make it into this sacred estate where glaciers finger down mountains, where rigid peaks glow with an inner light. I have infused every step up this mountain with symbolic hues. If Pamela were here, she wouldn't go; I'm certain of that. But some gender-specific, amniotic current pulls at me.

I see the disappointment in the eyes of those around me, especially Steph. Having just graduated with her doctorate in immunology from Columbia University, she is taking a hiatus before heading for post-doc work at Harvard. And she is here to think about life's choices. She loves the mountains, and in fact divorced her husband partly because he didn't share her enthusiam for hikes in the New England hills. Yet she is on the verge of committing to the indoor life of academia. Maybe, she has wondered aloud, she could become a mountain guide instead.

Steph is strong, and has consistently been at the front of the pack as we trekked over the past week. I enjoy her company. So in the cold moments of silence after Maureen's presentation, I wander over to Steph and lean to her ear conspiratorially: "Why don't you ask Maureen if you can join me? You're strong. You can do it. Tell her I asked if you would go with me." Steph stares at me with surprise; then a look of excitement

THE HIMALAYA ARE AN OPEN BOOK OF GEOLOGICAL STRUCTURES AND PROCESSES, AND THERE IS NO BETTER PLACE TO WITNESS SUCH A WIDE RANGE AS IN THE ANNAPURNA REGION AT DAWN.

sweeps across her face. She dashes to Maureen for a consult. Minutes later she returns. She will be joining the expedition. But the box is now opened, and next in line is Elise. The daughter of Archie and Theresa, Elise is twenty-two, yet looks sixteen, with a delicate, pale face, a slight body, and a shy demeanor. She is extra-sensitive to the sun and always wears a wide-brimmed floppy hat, carries an umbrella, and wraps her hands inside her long-sleeved shirt. Yet, she, too, has been a strong hiker, usually just a few paces behind Steph and myself, and sometimes up front. So when Elise hears that Steph and I have been granted exemptions, she broaches the same request with Maureen. "No, I'm sorry. No more. Besides, young people are more prone to altitude sickness," Maureen replies. She then retells the story of one memorable client, Gilbert, who insisted on going higher despite her warnings, and was carried down the mountain on her back with cerebral edema. Elise turns away to the Modi Khola River and cries. Theresa grows angry and questions the preferential treatment; the group dynamic disintegrates.

But by now I am gone, heading up the incline behind Ngati, with Steph in tow. Behind her trails a stray Tibetan mastiff, who adopted us at our Bamboo campsite. Dawa Lama, our thirty-nine-year-old cook and a veteran of sixteen years of trekking, will meet us later, after fetching some of our necessary camping gear. We've gone only a few steps when a young, white-faced Englishman carrying a sleeping bag under his arm comes scrambling down the trail. "Don't go any farther," he implores. "An ice chunk

"NAMASTE," OFFERS A BOY FROM THE VILLAGE OF GHANDRUK (6,000 FEET).

came down and just missed me. My three friends kept going, and they're crazy. I almost died…"

This is not soothing news, but Ngati says he knows a way around this one avalanche spot, and that we can advance cautiously. So up we go, into a dark cloud. As we approach the first swath of avalanche debris, we see a message scrawled in the snow: No Pass. But Ngati's inborn system computes the distance across, the freshness of the snow, and the angle of the sun, and he is willing to proceed. The rubble at our feet is from an avalanche a few days old, he tells us. It looks like someone rolled a bin of soccer balls off the ridge. The trail completely disappears into this white riot of ice and snow. Ngati instructs us to loosen our backpacks, so we can jettison them if another avalanche begins, and urges us to cross over, if we can, in a *lung-gom* mode, a type of Tibetan mystic running. Our scramble across looks more like pink-skinned tourists headed for happy hour.

A STRONG RELIGIOUS HERITAGE PERMEATES THE PHYSICAL AND CULTURAL LANDSCAPE IN THE ANNAPURNA REGION. TEMPLES, SHRINES, FLAGS, AND PRAYER WALLS MARK THE ENTRANCES AND EXITS TO VILLAGES. HERE, RELIGION IS NOT JUST A PHILOSOPHY BUT A WAY OF LIFE. STARTING AT A YOUNG AGE, MOST FOLLOW SOME FORM OF HINDUISM OR BUDDHISM, OFTEN BLENDED WITH INDIGENOUS SHAMANISTIC BELIEFS AND SUPERSTITIONS.

When the trail reappears it sneaks beneath an overhanging wall. As we start toward it, the unsullied oxygen of this space splits with a rumble, and a spume of ice and snow spills off the rim like a white waterfall, right onto the path. "Sir, that's where the Englishman was almost hit," Ngati says. "And two years ago a German was caught by an avalanche here and died. But I have another way." Ngati steers us off the trail, into knee-deep snow. We cross to the east side of the river and up a small rise, out of the immediate way of the avalanches that spill down from Hiunchuli, the dripping mountain we can't see that towers over the western walls of the Modi Khola. As we wade upwards we can see and hear spears of lethal ice dropping on the path not taken.

After a couple hours of hard trekking we can see Bagar and its one building, the Gangapurna Lodge, named for the 24,458-foot-high mountain that looms directly to the north, which in turn is named for another Hindu goddess. From our chilly aerie the scene below looks like a Christmas card of an Idaho hunting lodge surrounded by snow-draped birch and hemlocks. As we ease down the hill's sharp cleavage, Steph slips and begins to slide toward the edge. Ngati grabs her, and is dragged along a few feet, but arrests the fall at the edge.

At last, we cross the river and step our way up to the red-lumber lodge, the last outpost before the Sanctuary. We are at 10,825 feet. At half-past noon we open the door and discover three other visitors and the innkeeper inside. The foreigners are Nick and Nicolette, both from England, and Shelva from Israel, all with lusciously dressed accents and all terribly unprepared for a mountain expedition. None has gaiters or waterproof outerwear, and khaki-haired Nick has made it to this spot wearing shorts. Because of its usually easy access to the high mountains, the Annapurna massif has become the most popular trekking region in Nepal, with three times as many annual tourists as the Mount Everest area. In fact, there are more foreign trekkers, some fifty thousand last year, than there are villagers in the region. Probably at this moment, downstream from our roost, several hundred trekkers are biding time, wandering around, or retreating. Here at Bagar we are the vanguard, the last of the salmon swimming upstream. Nobody is out front, save two lodge owners reportedly stuck at the 13,000-foot-high Annapurna Base Camp. And so our little den has a vaguely exclusive air, dark and sumptuous with plight.

As Steph and I settle in and order a yak cheese pizza, we hear what sounds like the low peal of organ music outside. Another avalanche. And the weather is getting nastier. Faint crow's feet nest under Ngati's chocolate eyes as he announces we won't continue farther today. In fact, he says he must head back to the main group. "You're an experienced mountaineer. Why don't you stay with us?" I appeal. "I'm sorry, sir," he answers. "I have four children now. I do not take those risks anymore." And with that, Ngati, lean and brown and as hard-muscled as a snow leopard, disappears into the whiteness.

We try to relax in this little outpost, and hope for better weather tomorrow. Shelva pulls out a pack of Camel cigarettes and a deck of cards, and we settle back for an

S TEEP AND UNSTABLE, THE HIMALAYA CONTINUES TO BE UPLIFTED, COMPRESSED, AND
FOLDED TODAY. THE FORCES OF NATURE ARE CONSTANTLY SCULPTING: THE
GLACIERS CARVE, SMOOTH, AND POLISH; EARTHQUAKES TRIGGER LANDSLIDES
AND AVALANCHES THAT SHEER MOUNTAINSIDES; AND RAINS WASH AWAY THOU-
SANDS OF TONS   OF TOPSOIL.

afternoon of hot lemon and Hearts. Just when Nick is shooting the moon, Dawa arrives, unobtrusive as the wind slipping through the door. Through a weak smile he tells us the weather stinks.

With the dark, we step outside for the short walk past the sleeping mastiff to the frigid meat-locker barracks of the Gangapurna Lodge. There is no electricity here, so no reading lamp. I pull an egg-shaped novelty candle from my pack and light it to postpone the day's finish, and to read a card unrolled from my sleeping bag, a ritual I've performed every night. Pamela secretly buried a stack of greeting cards in my bag, one for each night of my trek. I pull out this one and read it: "Have a safe, sublime, sweet, serene, sure, and sacred trip." It is a warm moment that stays with me as I crawl into my sleeping bag, where I repeat my nightly mantra: "I hope I don't see Pamela this week."

The morning doesn't look much prettier, the sky like under-exposed Ektachrome with snow slightly buzzing around. Even our Tibetan mastiff has abandoned us, probably for better climes downhill. Dawa casts aspersions as I finish my three-egg omelette, reminding me that three days ago we passed the rock shrine to Pujinim Barahar, the powerful mountain goddess who protects the Annapurna Sanctuary. Beyond the shrine, no impure person should pass, and no polluting foods, such as eggs, are allowed. Violations risk the anger of the goddess, whose revenge will be sickness or death. In 1956, when Colonel James O.M. "Jimmy" Roberts became the first outsider to enter this sacred ground, he left fifty eggs behind at the shrine. I apologize to Dawa, but inside I remind myself I don't subscribe to such myths.

Dawa recommends we wait a couple hours before heading out. Our plan is to see if we can march the two hours or so through the pinched gateway of the sanctuary to the Machapuchare Base Camp. We know the camp is abandoned and closed, but it's where we might rest before heading west another few hours through waist-high snow to our ultimate target, the Annapurna Base Camp. There we could join the two hunkered-down lodge owners for the night, then retreat from the sanctuary the following day.

So we while away the morning with more card games. Then, around noon, the sun finally breaks through and the world is briefly bent toward us. We all rush outside to witness the scene, a view up valley of Gangapurna's triangular snow-and-rock face. Pastel waves of light cascade off the sharp walls, and the world pulses with possibilities. This is our chance. We hoist our packs and head out into the snow, up to where the mountains blush, toward the vestibule of the otherwise impregnable sanctuary.

After forty-five minutes trudging through the snow, Steph stops, leans down, and picks up a lone black feather from a cinereous vulture, a bird seemingly as out of place at this altitude and landscape as us. Minutes later we reach the remains of a huge, recently triggered avalanche. It is several hundred yards wide, and, like a huge, pocked arm, it reaches all the way across the Modi Khola to the far wall of the ravine. Upstream, less than a mile away, we can see the point where the trail squeezes through the steep-walled pass to Annapurna Sanctuary's restricted precincts. The Gurungs, the Sino-Tibetan ethnic group that has lived in the shadows of the Annapurna for thousands of years, believe

this is the abode of Pujinim Barahar, the goddess who protects the Annapurna Sanctuary. The Tibetans, who view the range from the other side, say this is the home of Tara, the Savioress of Tibetan Buddhism.

Then, as Dawa, Steph, and I stare into the chalky abyss of the avalanche, something roars behind us, and we turn to see a shower of snow spraying off the east rim directly above Nick, Nicolette, and Shelva, who are a few minutes

LESS THAN A MILE AWAY IS THE POINT WHERE THE TRAIL SQUEEZES THROUGH THE STEEP-WALLED VESTIBULE TO THE ANNAPURNA SANCTUARY'S RESTRICTED PRECINCTS.

behind us. Nick, a skittish man to begin with, runs in circles with the noise, and then makes a series of superhuman flying leaps through the snow back toward the lodge. But the avalanche never materializes; it peters out a hundred yards short of our companions, and Dawa laughs out loud at the spectacle. It breaks the tension, but only for a moment.

By the time Nick and his friends reach us, Dawa's face is again a map of worries. The sky has darkened and boxed us in once more, and the Himalayan wind is whistling. "What is ahead if we cross this avalanche?" I ask Dawa. "There are at least three more this size between here and the Machapuchare Base Camp," he explains, "and new ones could fall at any moment. The mountain sets the rules here. What you just heard and saw was not a real avalanche. A real one sounds like a big plane crashing, and all you can do is put your hands over your face to keep a breathing pocket as you're buried. And

MOST EXPERTS ESTIMATE THAT THE HIMALAYA IS APPROXIMATELY FORTY MILLION YEARS OLD— QUITE YOUNG IN TERMS OF MOUNTAIN SYSTEMS. MOVING IMPERCEPTIBLY NORTHWARDS FOR THOUSANDS OF YEARS, THE INDIAN SUBCONTINENT EVENTUALLY COLLIDED WITH THE EURASIAN LANDMASS, COMPRESSING THE OCEAN THAT LAY IN BETWEEN INTO GEOLOGICAL BEDS AND THRUSTING THEM UPWARD WITH CONTINUING FORCE.

hope someone finds you. Eighteen months ago, just a little farther up this valley, we lost a porter to an avalanche. This is a very dangerous passage."

"Can we keep going?" I ask.

"I don't think so. The weather is getting worse. It is too dangerous. We should go back and wait until tomorrow."

It seems we're standing at the threshold between the ordinary universe and the *Bardo*, a sacred realm, and I have a powerful urge to continue, powered by a belief that this mission is more than just a hike. I consider ignoring Dawa. It looks as though I could dash across this avalanche track and continue upwards to the womb of the sanctuary in minutes. In normal conditions, the lodges at the Annapurna Base Camp are less than four hours away. But now it would take significantly longer, the risks are quite high, and I did promise Maureen I would abide by Dawa's orders. Besides, if Pamela is home, as I hope she is, I know I really should not run the risk of continuing.

So we retreat, crossing Nick's forty-leagues-apart bootprints, where he leaped away from the runty avalanche. Once back at the lodge, we settle in for more card games, more hot lemon, a few rounds of international Scrabble, and watch the wretched weather grow worse.

At nightfall I light my egg candle and lie awake in my sleeping bag for hours. Perhaps it is the altitude, perhaps the frustration bends, but it is also thoughts of Pamela. A week ago she would have heard the news. And if the word was wrong, I might see her in a couple of days. I so hope not. At last the candle flickers and goes out.

When I get up to relieve myself around midnight, I step outside into the snow and see a sky so clear the starlight casts shadows on Machapuchare. So many sparkles and glitters and glints appear above me it looks like an expensive bauble was dropped and shattered in heaven. I stand transfixed, shivering in silent wonder. Maybe the morning will be kind, and luck will get me up into the space of the sanctuary.

Sometime before dawn I awake to the ear-rending explosion of a 747 crashing. And then another. And another. The clamor seems to be coming from down valley, toward the Himalaya Hotel, where the rest of our group is camping, waiting for us. It was next to the Himalaya Hotel in the spring of 1989 that three Sherpa kitchen boys died when an avalanche rolled over their tent in the middle of the night. I

Young Tibetan refugee Buddhists in a temple outside Pokhara, the hilltown where treks begin up into the Annapurna Sanctuary.

get up to relieve myself once again and step out into a blizzard. The sky has shut, flakes are flying, and almost a foot of fresh snow smothers the landscape. I cast about for the skyline, an outline, any line, but there is only whiteness in the roaring dark. I know now I am not going to make it to the oval-shaped cul-de-sac called the Annapurna Sanctuary.

An hour later we gather for a solemn breakfast before heading back down the hill. Dawa tells us that two years ago an avalanche from Machapuchare rolled down and ripped the roof off the Gangapurna Hotel in Bagar, where at this moment we are feeling so protected. Minutes after his story, we hear another cataclysmic roar, and a blast of wind pushes its way through the cracks, lifts up the side of the roof a few inches, powdering us with snow and forcing us to shut our eyes. A scream follows from outside. In runs Nicolette, pasted with snow and looking like the abominable snow-woman. She was

THE ANNAPURNA HIMAL IS THE THRONEROOM OF THE MOUNTAIN GODDESSES. IT WAS THE DESTINATION OF THE FIRST AMERICAN WOMEN'S EXPEDITION TO AN 8,000-METER-HIGH PEAK IN 1978.

on the "seat of government," as the Dawa calls the loo, when we were blasted; fortunately, it was from an avalanche several hundred yards down the valley and we just felt the collateral effects. It brings the point home, however. It is time to head back. Even the innkeeper of the Gangapurna Lodge announces he is leaving his place of business, and will head down with us.

So up we suit and down we go, wading through hip-deep snow, searching for signs of a path.

Within minutes we encounter the shattered cascade of snow and ice that is an avalanche aftermath, likely the one that blasted our lodge over breakfast. About fifty yards wide, it looks like someone dumped hundreds of truckloads of frozen margaritas over the rim. Dawa tells us to do our best to run across. He goes first, picking his way across the

A BRIDGE ACROSS THE MODI KHOLA RIVER, WHICH DRAINS THE HIGH PEAKS OF THE ANNAPURNA RANGE.

blocky ruins of ice crystals. Then I watch as Steph takes a deep breath and follows, looking as though she's running on stilts. I jump in right behind, and up and down we scramble over the jumble. Then, as Steph is climbing the last wall of the avalanche gully, she falls back toward me. I push her upwards, my hands on her back, while Dawa reaches down and grabs her jacket. For a moment we hang there, balanced on the edge, then together, in a single hump, we roll up and out of the gully and onto the untracked snow.

"What happened?" I ask Steph, who sits down and gasps a few breaths. "I have to confess," she pants. "I have an acute phobia for avalanches. I tried to hold my breath while crossing the avalanche, and I couldn't do it. I almost blacked out."

I don't know whether to praise Steph for her bravery or chastise her. Either is pointless at the moment. We have to get down the mountain. Dawa said that most avalanches occur between 9 A.M. and 2 P.M., when the sun is most intense, melting the new snow and triggering falls. Now it is almost 9:30, and we have hours to go to reach the Himalaya Hotel.

From Bagar to Deurali (10,600 feet), the next notch on the ladder down the mountain, we cross four more fresh avalanche sweeps, then a huge one before Hinku Cave, then another before we walk into the empty grounds of the Himalaya Hotel. Maureen and our group abandoned the spot this morning, as have all guests, the lodge owners, and employees. The only living being is Ngati, who stayed behind to check on our safety. So with one more in our expedition, we continue down a trail that tunnels through dense forests of bamboo surrealistically covered with snow. It is a beautiful sight, and for a second I wish Pamela were here to share it with me. Then I catch myself, and erase that thought.

Another hour of walking and we reach Doban (8,550 feet), where we meet the first tourists we've seen in a couple days, including a group led by a famous British trekker, Keith Miller. While his six guests are huddled in the cook tent over a Scrabble board, Keith intercepts us with an offer of black tea. He tells us that in his years of wanderings in the Himalayas he's never seen a storm of this magnitude this time of year. I tell him a bit about the "storm of the century," which hit the East Coast of the U.S. just as I was leaving for Nepal, and wonder if we're in the middle of some sort of global weather change. But Keith reminds me that the Gurung people have long said the erosion of religious customs brought about by foreign tourism has angered the guardian spirit Pujinim Barahar, and in retaliation she has brought bad luck, bad harvests, and, increasingly, bad weather.

"Aren't you worried camping this close to the avalanches?" I finally ask Keith. "No," he answers. "I know this area. We're safe here. We're not going up any farther, but this spot is okay." We bid one another good luck and goodbye, and I fall back into line behind the descending Dawa.

But a few minutes down the snowslope the loudest boom yet rends the air, like a squadron of F-16s crashing. The sound rolls through the mountains. We look up the blue-fogged valley and see a mushroom cloud erupt hundreds of feet into the sky. The Gurungs tell of columns of smoke seen rising from Machapuchare, and believe it is incense being offered by the meditating Shiva. This seems more like nuclear disaster.

When the silence returns it is so deep it rings. It seems as though the mountain has inhaled and is holding its breath. Finally the quiet is interrupted as a young French girl sprints down the trail, pale-faced and panicked. "What happened?" I call out. "It just missed me," she exclaims. "I was crossing an avalanche field and suddenly I heard the noise. I ran and it came down and just missed me. It ripped away the tents of two Germans." "What about the Brits?" I ask, as she blurs by.

"I don't know," she blurts, and hastens down the trail as though pursued by a ghost. We decide to pause for a drink, and see if any news is forthcoming, and sure enough, minutes later Keith Miller and his group emerge, exhausted and frightened. A young woman with big eyes pours out the story: "We were all in the cook tent playing Scrabble when we heard the noise. Keith ran in and told us to run for the tea house two hundred yards away, and as we did a cloud of snow blasted our camp. It was from an avalanche just up the valley from us. It flattened all our tents, and picked up the cook tent where we had been, and

tossed it three hundred yards away, into the river. But, when it was over, we went back to where the tent had been and the table was still standing and the Scrabble board, with all the letters in place, was still on top. Keith had us abort the game, though, and head for low ground...and I was this close to a nine-letter word."

Campsites on the Annapurna trek are so scenic they seem to be situated on holy ground.

We have to keep going, too, if we want to reach the hill town of Chomrong by nightfall, where Ngati says our group is waiting. So we stride down through Tolkienesque forests of brilliantly flowering rhododendron and oak, down to the village of Bamboo (7,700 feet), where we pass a local family warming itself in the communal rubbish pit outside the lodge; down the winding trail to the wobbly suspension bridge across the Chomrong Khola River; and finally up some 3,465 uneven flagstone steps to our campsite. We've been hiking ten hours straight, and my brain is all blisters. We've covered the same distance that took four days on the upward journey. "Happy birthday," I call to Theresa Blackburn as we hobble up the last pitch into camp on feet that have lost all feeling. Maureen runs over, gives us big hugs, and tells us how worried she's been. But I have other things on my mind. I look around to see if Pamela is in camp, and am relieved to see she isn't. By my calculations, she would have caught up with our group by now if things had gone wrong, so I am relieved—and hopeful. Maureen sends me to consult with a glass of rakshi, and minutes later I am collapsed in my tent. My skin no longer knows whether to feel flushed or chilled, as my energy has lapsed while the internal heat somehow carries on.

At 11:00 P.M., I am punched awake by the roar of another air crash, though this one sounds larger than anything before. Then the tent fills with the flicker of lightning, and there are more thunderous cracks and reverberations. It's not the mountain, it's the sky talking this time, in a different language—a thunderstorm. Then I hear singing from a nearby tent. I can't place the voice. I slide back into a heavy sleep.

The light the next morning is commanding and bright, the finest yet, and out my tent door I can see the elegant blade of the 22,943-foot-high Machapuchare, the fish-tail mountain whose form explains its name; and the back-of-a-sperm whale summit of Annapurna South, 23,607 feet high. Nothing grows up there, but the sparkling peaks look alive, inviting, ready for a hike. Maybe things will work out after all.

Our goal is the village of Ghandruk (6,600 feet), the headquarters for the five-hundred-square-mile region known as ACAP, or the Annapurna Conservation Area Project, an ambitious plan that hopes to integrate the preservation policies of a national park with the wants and needs of the local peoples. As we travel we're back on the tourist route now, the Coke Route some call it, because there's a spot to buy Coca Cola at almost every twist in the trail. Ngati carries a whistle he says he uses for traffic jams along this pedestrian route. But the new knots of trekkers don't bother me, nor does the fact that I didn't plant any seeds in the Annapurna Sanctuary. I'm satisfied in surviving the avalanches, and knowing that Pamela is not here.

And so I walk blithely along, skirting sculpted fields of millet and corn, admiring the windflowers, breathing Daphne's perfume, and absorbing a perfect day of life and abundance under the Annapurna Range. Then, around three in the afternoon, just a mile short of the slate-roofed houses of Ghandruk, I round a corner, and there on a rock is Pamela. She jumps down to the trail and wraps her arms around me. I squeeze back and, with a terrific wrench, the whole universe flips over in the pit of my stomach. I collapse into a flood of tears that adds to the rapids of the Modi Khola. Her presence means the IUI didn't work.

After ten years of almost nonstop travel and adventure together, we recently recognized we may have missed our chance to realize a common goal: to have a child. The doctor told us the clock might have ticked too long; we were both in our forties. However, there was one last chance. By using fertility drugs and an intrauterine insemination procedure (IUI), the reproductive endocrinologist estimated a 4 percent chance of pregnancy. That was enough to get our hopes up. We agreed that after the insemination, I would leave for a woman's place, Annapurna, and she would stay behind to finish her tests. On March 19 an ultrasound would reveal the verdict. If it were positive, I would come home to an impending family, and a lifelong goal realized for both of us. If the test proved negative, Pamela would hop a jet to Kathmandu the next day and try to find me in the Himalayas. We had both hoped she would miss that flight.

The views are spectacular the next several days. We wander among the terraced foothills, beneath the snowy shoulders of Annapurna, sharing thoughts and trying to deconstruct the Buddhist abstraction that to want something more is the beginning of an end to happiness. But another thought still echoes among these hard silver hills: to want nothing else is the end of all beginnings. Maybe Annapurna is an illustration of Plato's "ideal form" of a peak. A thing to be scaled, a manifestation of the unattainable, existing as a perpetual destination, or not at all. And trekking isn't required to plant a flag, or a seed, on top.

THE ELEGANT BLADE OF THE 22,943-FEET-HIGH MACHAPUCHARE. TO PRESERVE THE MOUNTAIN'S SANCTITY, IT IS OFF-LIMITS TO CLIMBERS.

To reach Pokhara, the end of the Annapurna trek, we have to go up again before we can descend. That path, we know, marks the way to new altitudes and concepts, and another irresistible mountain.

From a certain point onward, there is no longer any turning
back. That is the point that must be reached.

—FRANZ KAFKA

THE ATLAS:
TRAVELS WITH
A MULE

The music of the oud goes on, a patterned background for our aimless talk. Listening to its notes is like watching the smoke of a wood fire curl and fold in untroubled air.

Pamela and I are in the restaurant of the Le Tichka Salam Marrakech Hotel in the middle of Marrakech. Worn from travel, we linger over the last of our Toulal Guerrouane, a tired Moroccan red wine. Several cats are sprawled around the room, in positions that mirror our mood. With muted interest we both look up when the waiter pours a cup of sugared mint tea, deftly cascading the brew from three feet above the table. An idea strikes.

"Let's go have tea in the Sahara," I suggest, looking into Pamela's dark eyes, which brighten with the prospect.

It seems a logical notion, as close as it is. But there is one small problem: the great fence of the Atlas Mountains, which separates the upper body of Africa from the Sahara. We could drive over one of the several passes, but that wouldn't be sporting. After some discussion, we decide to trek over the great range, north to south, to the burning sands.

CREATED BY THE SAME GLOBAL CONVULSIONS THAT SHAPED THE ALPS AND THE HIMALAYAS, THE PERPETUALLY SNOW-CAPPED ATLAS RISE TO MORE THAN 13,000 FEET. HERE, WE ARE NEGOTIATING THE CENTRAL HIGH ATLAS DOWN INTO THE BOUGUEMEZ VALLEY.

At peace in prayer. Five times a day the Berbers, who are Muslim, face Mecca and offer their prayer to Allah.

The sedimentary Bouguemez Valley is richly fertile and supports twenty-five villages and hundreds of sheep.

The next day, at the offices of Atlas Sahara Treks, owner Bernard Fabry unrolls a map on his desk, then traces a route with his finger through the Central High Atlas. If we take a four-wheel-drive vehicle we could crawl up the Aroudane Mountain and drop down the other side into the Bouguemez Valley, the end of the road. From there we could trek for four days over the Mgoun pass to the other side. We would reach the road, where we could hire a vehicle to take us to Ouarzazate, the gateway to the Sahara. Bernard would set us up with a guide from the Bouguemez Valley. "But, I must warn you," Bernard says in his heavy latté accent, "the weather this time of year is quite unpredictable. Once in the mountains, if a storm comes in you could be stranded for days, even weeks."

In *Metamorphoses*, Ovid recounts the Roman myth that explained the creation of the Atlas Mountains: "Atlas was all at once a mountain, beard and hair were forests, and his arms and shoulders were mountain ridges; what had been his head was the peak of a mountain, and his bones were boulders."

Groggy and feeling guilty for being a few minutes late, we stumble into the lobby of the Hotel El Andalous at 6:10 A.M. An hour later our guide arrives along with a new Land Rover Defender. He is twenty-two-year-old Rachid Mousklou, who has studied geology for two years at the University of Marrakech, and recently, when not guiding,

GUIDE RACHID MOUSKLOU, WEARING HIS *CHECHIA*, LOOKS OVER AT THE BOUGUEMEZ VALLEY (WHERE HE WOULD RATHER BE).

has been teaching other guides about the rocks and the birds in the region. He is in some demand, as he speaks five languages: English, German, French, Arabic, and Berber. He has the glassy back eyes of a doll, with little expression (accentuated by his hat) and an arched forehead. Five hours later we are wending our way up the juniper-lined mountain, surging into the snow line. We lunch at the Tizi n' Tirghist pass (2,629 feet), then begin the long descent into the Bouguemez Valley. The landscape is denuded, most of the trees felled long ago by Berber women collecting firewood. Occasionally, though, we pass a replanting grove filled with young black cyprus, often topped by magpies that share the same dull color of the mountains' south side.

Our first Berber encounter is in the village of Iframe, where Mohammed, a friend of Rachid's, bounds out to greet us in his Air Mowabs, a pair of Levis, a fleece jacket, and the same arched face. He invites us inside for some sweet tea and flinty exchanges with Rachid we can't comprehend.

An hour later we continue our journey to the sole hotel in the valley, the Dar Itarane (House of Stars), in the mud-walled village of Imelghas. It is a lovely and lonely place, and because it is December, we are the only guests. We stake out a spot in the large dinning room, beneath a cedar ceiling encircled by verses from the Koran, and in front of the fireplace. This will be our base camp.

CHILDREN OF THE ATLAS. PERSONAL POSSESSIONS ARE FEW HERE; THEIR
GREATEST ASSET IS A SMILE.

IN THE HOPI-LIKE VILLAGE OF TALAT RIGHANE, THE LOW OCHER-COLORED HOUSES SEEM
TO REFLECT THEIR INHABITANTS' SKIN COLOR IN THE LATE AFTERNOON SUN.

MARRAKECH, GATEWAY TO THE ATLAS AND JUST AN HOUR'S DRIVE AWAY, IS AS RICH AND GARISH AS THE MOUNTAINS ARE SPARE AND UNPRETENTIOUS.

That evening, over oily vegetable soup and lumps of half-cooked lamb fat, Rachid tells us he has been speaking to the villagers. He says they recommend we don't attempt the Mgoun Pass. It is too dangerous this time of year, the weather too unpredictable. He suggests we hike in the other direction, to his father's valley, as an alternative. I unroll the map, trace the intended route for Rachid, and tell him I think we should give it a go. After all, I was an experienced professional guide, and if the conditions are deemed too dangerous, we'll simply turn around. I'm certain we can make it, I conclude.

Rachid looks at us. "Inscha'allah," he replies with a shrug, and leaves the room for the night.

Sharp morning light fills the room, the polished floor tiles reflecting the sun onto the ceiling as if they were water. After a breakfast of lemon grass tea and round bread, we decide to explore the valley and stretch our legs before attempting the first pass.

We wander among the fields of potatoes, apples, corn, and wheat, through several of the twenty-five villages in the valley. Rachid is our guide, but for someone so knowledgeable he is surprisingly reticent. He states the obvious, that the valley is sedimentary (my dear Watson), then leads us toward a dramatic swirl of earth that strategically overlooks the valley. We scratch our way up the steep mesa and into a two-hundred-year-old shrine, Sidi Moussa. It is an intriguing piece of architecture, cube-modular with several tortuous passageways. It has served multiple purposes, Rachid tells me when I ask directly. It was a watchtower, a winter storage bin, a grave site for the high and holy, and, most important, the home of a mountain god, a spirit who not only protects, but helps fertilize women.

According to legend, a woman who is having problems becoming pregnant must come to Sidi Moussa on three Thursday nights in a row and spend the night. On the fourth night she must bring a black sheep or other animal to sacrifice, and she will then find herself pregnant. Back in Marrakech, Bernard Fabry had told me of this myth, and said he thought there was a more simplistic explanation. He asked me to notice how similar everyone in the valley looked, and then to note the arched face of the caretaker at Sidi Moussa.

As we walk around the periphery of this belvedere, Rachid looks across the valley to Jbel Waogoulzat, the mountain we are scheduled to climb the next day. It looks like a knee drawn up under a huge sheet. With a staccato gesture he points to a faint zig-zag in the snow, says that is our trail, and grimaces.

We continue our hike to the valley's main village, Tabant, where a bar stands next to a former French administrative building. Outside a man sits on a white plastic chair, reading a paper, sipping a cup of tea. It looks very much like a scene outside any French café, only here the man's face is hidden deep in the recesseses of his pointed burnoose, looking like Alec Guinness in *Star Wars*. I wander in, and in front of a blaring TV

ONE OF THE WOMEN WHO BELONGS TO THE AITATTA TRIBE—A NOMADIC BERBER CONFEDERATION—IN HER TRADITIONAL DRESS.

THE TIZI-N-AIT IMI PASS, OR "THE PASS OF THE SHEEP WITH BLACK EYES." OUR MULE WITH NO NAME DOESN'T EVEN STOP TO ADMIRE THE VIEW.

a young child is watching a racy dance number on an Indian version of MTV. Over in the corner a group of teenagers is playing Foosball on a table on which the playing field is plastered with the famous nude shot of Marilyn Monroe that appeared in the first issue of *Playboy*.

That evening Rachid tells us a superstition in the valley holds that people sometimes turn into animals, and that his grandmother, who lived to be 110, was transformed into a mule. Then Rachid again tries to talk us out of attempting our journey, citing the weather. The weather has been fine, I point out, sunny and cloudless. What's the problem? Rachid sulks. I wonder if the animal transformation thing could be hereditary.

At daybreak we're up and packed, and in the compound is an eagle-faced man named Ahmed and his mule with no name. After he straps on our baggage, as well as food, cooking materials, and sleeping blankets, we head out. Rachid is silent as we make our way up a trail named "The Ambusher." This was one of the caravan passages that enabled the transport of dates, henna, gold, and salt between the Sahara and ports in the north. Slowly, we wind up the pass through several biblical-looking villages, where men with wrapped heads and flowing robes mill about in an ancient way, up through groves of juniper and into the snow, following in the footsteps of our nameless mule. The winter light is diffused and slanted, giving the landscape a New Mexican look. At one point

THE SPECTACULAR MGOUN VALLEY IS SO ISOLATED THAT NO FOREIGN POWER HAS
EVER PENETRATED IT.

RACHID MOUSKLOU LOOKS UP AT THE MGOUN MOUNTAINS HE REFUSES TO
EXPLORE ON THIS TREK.

the mule slips in the snow and almost falls. If the mule breaks a leg, he will have to be shot, and Ahmed would lose his greatest ass(et). This would not do, so Ahmed unloads the two largest bags and sets them in the snow. I wonder what his plan is as he continues up the hill, leaving behind two of my bags. It isn't until we are close to the crest that I realize my money, passport, and air tickets are in one of the bags left in the snow, and I feel a stab of panic. But I'm too exhausted to backtrack.

After six hours of continuous walking, we crest the Tizi-n-Ait Imi Pass, also known as "The Pass of the Sheep with Black Eyes," and are faced with the stunning white comb of the Mgoun, across the next valley. The wind is howling here, and as I pull on my wool hat, Rachid wraps his head in his blue *chechia*, a Berber head scarf. We all stoop behind a large rock and unpack our lunch; cheese, yellow apples, oily black olives, walnuts, hard-boiled eggs, and bread. While noshing, Rachid and Ahmed scramble back down the mountain, returning some minutes later with my missing bags on their shoulders. Then Rachid points to some clouds in the distance and somberly tells me, "I think we must go back. The clouds mean bad weather." But as I survey the sky I see that the clouds are in the north, while the wind is definitely blowing from the south, the direction we're headed. In fact, the sky ahead is a brilliant blue. "Rachid," I protest, "the clouds are behind us, and moving away. The weather looks fine in front. I say we should just keep going. How far to the village where we'll spend the night?"

"Four hours. But we shouldn't go on. It's too dangerous."

TWO YOUNG BOYS PAUSE, WHILE ASTRIDE THEIR MULE ON THE TRAIL.

What is his hidden agenda? "I insist. We can do it. There's no reason to turn back," I say, resolutely shouldering my pack and starting down the trail. With more reluctance than the mule, Rachid follows.

It's an easy descent into the Mgoun Valley, and soon we're walking alongside the crisp Mgoun River. In every direction the view is spectacular, like how I imagine James Hilton's Shangri-la. At one point we pass a series of caves across the river, with crude wooden ladders leading into the darkness. It looks like an Anasazi granary. An hour later we pass a fortress, Tighremt-n-Ait Ahmed, that guards the confluence of a tributary. Thirty

THE AMBUSHER TRAIL, WHICH WAS ONE OF THE CARAVAN PASSAGES THAT ALLOWED FOR THE TRANSPORT OF GOODS FROM THE SAHARA TO THE PORTS IN THE NORTH.

minutes later, we stumble into the Hopi-like village of Talat Righane, where the low ocher-colored houses seem to have sprung from the ground. We have entered another world. The people here are of the Aitatta tribe, a nomadic Berber confederation that wandered into this valley ages ago and stayed. All the men wear dun-colored burnooses. The women are intricately tattooed with indigo designs on their foreheads and henna-stained palms and fingers. Pendulum earrings of silver, turquoise, and amber swing as they walk and speak. As for clothing, they wear only black, blue, and red.

Rachid speaks with one of the village elders, and after a while we're led through a heavy wooden horseshoe-shaped door into a small compound, then up the stairs to a narrow room lined with Berber carpets and pillows. This will be our room, he indicates, and brings in a pile of blankets.

After settling in, we step outside to admire the landscape. It is the moment of twilight when light objects seem unnaturally bright, and the others restfully dark. Even in my pile sweater and North Face jacket, I still feel the cold, like a piece of metal inside me, yet the villagers, in their cotton clothes, don't seem to notice. One woman steps up to Rachid with her small son at her side, then pulls up the child's pant leg to reveal a festering wound the size of a half-dollar on his calf. "What is it?" I ask Rachid. "A dog bite," he replies with some disdain. There are a half-dozen Atlas sheepherder dogs within sight, a couple barking frenetically at our presence. "Well, isn't there a doctor she can see?" I ask.

"Not in this valley. She would have to climb over the pass to where we came from, but she won't because it would take two days, and she doesn't want to spend the money for the medicine."

"What about you? I saw you had a medical kit. Can you help?"

"Yes," Rachid says, but the woman and the small boy are already wandering away. "I'll look at the boy before we leave," he says, then turns on his heel toward the compound. The cold wind blows away the last feeble strands of light.

That night we huddle by a small propane lamp, extracting what little warmth it generates. Ahmed brings us tea and *tajine*, sliced vegetables and pieces of cartilaginous meat cooked over a wood fire, and we chow down. Then Rachid comes in and announces the latest news in his guttural mountain tone: "We can't go on. The villagers say the pass is closed, and it is impossible to proceed."

"Wait a minute. What about the Mgoun River? On the map there is a route that follows the river through a gorge and avoids the pass altogether. Why can't we try that?"

"That, too, is closed. It is impossible to pass this time of year. The water is too high."

"C'mon. This is December. This is the slowest time of year for runoff. We've seen the river; it's low, probably the lowest for the season."

"Well, the river in the gorge is still up to your chest, and the water is too cold now. We can't go on."

"Well, how about we just walk downstream tomorrow and check things out?"

After a long silence Rachid takes a draw on his Casa Sports cigarette, then replies, "Okay, but then we must turn back. You must promise me. We can always visit my father's valley."

Secretly I conspire to find someone in this valley with whom I can communicate, and get a second opinion. That will be tomorrow's agenda.

But it doesn't work as I hoped. Though I wander around without Rachid's company, but with my phrase books, it becomes apparent that nobody here speaks a word of French or Arabic. This is truly an isolated outpost. So much so, the French were never able to penetrate this valley. I don't see a single photograph of King Hassan II. It is the middle of December, and nobody here, I am certain, has ever heard of Christmas. Somehow I find that delightful, even though I cannot find a soul who can tell me if this journey can be completed. Finally, I begin to hike downstream in the direction of the gorge, with Rachid at my heels. At one point I pass several Berber women, as decorated as any I've seen, festooned with amber necklaces, their plaited hair shining with oil and flecked with safron. I pull out my camera to take a photo, and Rachid holds his hand up and stops me. "What's wrong?" I ask. "They believe you'll be taking their souls; or

they'll want money, and that's a bad habit." I can't argue with that, so I tuck my camera away and continue to hike.

Sometime in the early afternoon I hear the singing voices of women echoing up the canyon. We are entering the village of El Mrabitine, where Rachid had said the greatest singers in Morocco live. Soon we pass the women, who are in a harvest bent, swinging scythes in the fields. They look up as I pass, and I pull out my camera. They smile, and as Rachid is looking the other way, I click a few shots, then press a few dirham notes into the women's hands.

IN THE VILLAGE OF TABANT, A MAN IN A POINTED BURNOOSE READS HIS MORNING PAPER AS THOUGH IN A PARIS CAFE. THIS IS AS FAR AS THE FRENCH EVER INFILTRATED INTO THE HIDDEN VALLEYS OF THE HIGH ATLAS.

In this Old Testament village there is a single shop. Four men loiter out front, a Berber shop quartet. The store offers the usual items, and also a can of Coke, which I promptly buy. Then the shop owner, who has the applelike cheeks of a peasant, closes his shutter and leads us through a labyrinthine set of corridors up to a tea room, where he tears apart green stalks of mint and stuffs them into a little teapot. When Rachid wanders off for a few minutes, I desperately try to communicate with the shop owner, asking about the Mgoun Pass, about the river route, drawing pictures in my notebook. But he doesn't understand. When Rachid returns, I close my notebook and take a sip of tea.

"Are you certain we can't go forward?" I implore Rachid one last time, my voice rising. This exchange is becoming stylized and repetitive, like a belly dance. I suddenly feel a bit foolish with my oft-repeated question. In my twenties I, too, had been a guide, and one of the few unpleasant aspects of the job was having to deal with obnoxious clients who repeatedly demanded something impossible. For a second I am horrified to realize that, just as all children become their parents, I was becoming one of my clients.

"It's time to return," Rachid says after a time. It is getting late, and if we aren't going forward, we have to leave now to make it back to Talat Righana. But before we leave I walk down to the river. The air is heavy with the odor of spearmint that grows along the banks. I dip my hand in its waters. It is cold, and the volume has increased with several tributaries, so much so it looks like it might be navigated with a kayak or small raft. I find myself wishing I had somehow had the foresight to bring one. Then I could have paddled to the Sahara. I shrug, like Atlas, and turn to head home.

Along the way Rachid breaks his usual silence to tell me he hopes to one day visit the Andes. "What about Everest?" I ask. "No," he replies. "The Andes." Unusual, I think. Every other mountain guide I had ever met dreamed of visiting the Himalayas above all else.

The following day we stagger back into The House of Stars. The weather has been picture perfect, and I'm bitter and suspicious about whether we could have completed our journey. When I open my camera to change film, I discover that my roll did not advance, so the photos I took of the Berber women were never captured on film. The dining room, despite a blazing oak fire, seems stuffy and melancholy. Over couscous Rachid tells me that two Moroccan shepherds died trying to cross the Mgoun Pass just last month. He says they started their trek, travelling without mules, and it was a beautiful day. But a sudden storm came in at noon, and they froze to death. I don't know whether to believe him. The weather has been so ideal, and if we had continued we would be just one day from completing our crossing.

"By the way," I ask as he's leaving for bed. "Did you ever treat the boy with the dog bite?"

"No," he replies levelly, then disappears.

The next morning I awake to the sound of giant trees crashing. But that can't be right, because the few trees here are slight willows and poplars. I realize then it is thunder. I pull back the shutters. The sky is black and a huge storm has moved in. It's pouring rain, and lightning streaks across the sky. Fresh snow covers Jbel Waogoulzat, which I can barely make out across the valley. If we had continued, we would have been smack in the middle of this storm.

Four days later we find ourselves in a 1979 Mercedes 2000D taxi climbing the Tishka Pass on the way to Ouarzazate. The weather is still snotty, the storm releasing its last licks. Our driver/guide is Boukhriss A. Majid, a thin thirty-two-year-old playwright and mountain guide with a salient nose. He is everything Rachid is not: blithe, informative, passionate. He recites poetry and shares history as we wend up through the Atlas the easy way. At the top of the pass two tourist buses swerved on the ice and now block

the way. It looks as though we'll have to turn back, our journey thwarted once again. While waiting by a roadside stand selling red onyx and geodes, a little Berber girl wrapped in a shawl plasters me with a snowball and yells through a satisfied smile, "I'm Saddam Hussein; you George Bush." Finally, after a couple hours of digging, pushing, yelling, and shoveling sand under the wheels, the buses are freed, and the pass reopens.

THE GREAT FENCE OF THE ATLAS MOUNTAINS ARCS 1,500 MILES FROM THE ATLANTIC TO THE MEDITERRANEAN, SEPARATING THE UPPER BODY OF AFRICA FROM THE SAHARA.

We coil down into a dull rose landscape, past ruined casbahs, past caravans of women, who are bent over double as they carry their loads of firewood, their faces seamed with fatigue. And we pass a mule, its back piled high with lumpy, closed sacks, loping down the mountain.

Under a lowering sky, we drive through the stout, crenellated walls of the four-star Riam Salam hotel in Ouarzazate, and take a room that sits on the flat roof. From here we can see the sullen sweep of the desert, the date palms, the shimmering waters of a river that will never see the sea. I check my map, and find that the currents of the Mgoun River, which I had touched just a few days before, spill into the Dades, which in turn is a tributary of the Draa River, which flows by our hotel. We are reunited. And as a white crescent moon begins its rise to swim upwards, the waiter brings us our order on an ornate brass tray. And in the soft air we sip hot tea on the edge of the Sahara.

The day breaks and asks me: "Do you hear
the lingering water,
the water,
over Patagonia?"
and I reply: "Yes, I hear it."

—PABLO NERUDA, "I Awaken Suddenly in the
Night Thinking about the Far South"

Patagonia:
under the horns
of a dilemma

In faraway places, there are often familiar faces. I thought I recognized his movements, the nape of his neck. Hesitantly, I walked across the floor of the Carlos Ibanez Airport, in Punta Arenas, the sandy point at the tip of South America on the Strait of Magellan. He turned and it was him, it was Frenchy, a veteran adventure guide I had recruited into the fold so many years ago. We shared a guide hug, characterized by hearty slaps and exaggerated gestures, and simultaneously asked the same question: "What are you doing here?" He had just completed a trek through Western Patagonia; I was just arriving for the same. "Did you hear the news?" he asked. "The boat that crosses Lago Grey just sank; thirty people almost drowned." At first I was alarmed, but then I felt a twinge of resentment. Just a few days before, Leo LeBon, the seasoned Patagonian explorer, had unrolled a map in his Berkeley living room. He pulled his finger across Largo Grey and announced that with the new boat now in use one could reach the famous Grey Glacier in minutes, rather than the several days it took by foot. That was good news, I felt, as I had less time than I wanted to explore this landscape on the cone of the southern continent.

While I was still digesting the news, the boarding call for Frenchy's flight came. As he pulled on his pack he said, "I would never cross

The Torres del Paine, the impossibly vertical spires sculpted by twelve million years of ice and wind at the bottom of the South American continent.

▲ 163 ▲

THE TORRES DEL PAINE—A GIGANTIC BUBBLE OF ONCE-MOLTEN GRANITE THAT ROSE FROM THE CENTER OF THE EARTH LONG AGO AND WAS LATER COVERED WITH LARGE GLACIERS THAT CAME STREAMING OFF THE CONTINENTAL ICECAP DURING THE LAST ICE AGE.

THE REGAL ANDEAN CONDORS ARE COMMON IN THE PARK. THE WORLD'S LARGEST FLYING BIRDS, THEY EFFORTLESSLY RIDE THE WIND CURRENTS AROUND THE PEAKS AND TOWERS ON THEIR TWELVE-FOOT WINGSPANS.

THE THREE MAIN TOWERS LOOK LIKE COLOSSAL CRYSTALS GROWING SIDE BY SIDE.

In Torres del Paine National Park, the weather is "latitude with an attitude"—51 degrees south, with winds blowing north from Antarctica.

Icebergs continually calve from Grey Glacier into the waters of Lago Grey, where the boating accident occurred.

that lake on a boat. It's too dangerous." I thought the words odd, coming from an adventure guide, one who had rowed some of the biggest rapids in the world.

I walked to the parking lot, climbed into the back of a Ford Club Wagon, and started up the Carretera Austra. Though the van was barely three months old, the windshield was cracked and scratched from the hard driving here. The ride was rough, the scenery bleak and monotonous, and I managed to nod off. I awoke almost three hours later as we reached the halfway point, the fishing village of Puerto Natales, on the shores of Seno Ultima Esperanza (Last Hope Sound). Black-necked swans were gaggling in front of the ocean-side cafe where we parked. Inside, a bespectacled, pony-tailed pirate sat hunched over the table. He was Arian Manchego, twenty-eight years old, half

WHERE THE ANDES' FIVE-THOUSAND-MILE-LONG CHAIN OF MOUNTAINS COMES TO AN ABRUPT END AND PLUNGES INTO THE STORMY SOUTH PACIFIC, RISES THE PAINE RANGE—A SPECTACULAR ARRAY OF HUGE SPIRES AND SHARP PEAKS WITH SMOOTH WALLS RISING FOR 6,000 VERTICAL FEET OUT OF THE UNDULATING PATAGONIAN GRASSLANDS.

Peruvian, half Belgian and the chief guide for the explora, en Patagonia lodge in Torres del Paine National Park, the half-million-acre park and UNESCO biosphere reserve that

They ride like the wind along the Rio Paine near the Guarderia Laguna Amarga, an entrance to the national park.

was our ultimate destination. Over an avocado sandwich I asked if he had heard anything about the Lago Grey boat. He bellowed the laugh of a big-bellied bartender but then suddenly went graven, and the blood seemed to drain from his face.

He began recounting the events leading to the accident, which had happened three days before on Sunday, January 30. It was his first charter on the boat, which had just started service the week before. He was guiding a group of twenty-four senior citizens—he guessed the average age to be 60—who had just completed an Antarctica cruise and were enjoying a rest day before heading home. It was to be a two-hour cruise. While returning from Grey Glacier, the winds picked up and the lake was choppy with five-foot-high whitecaps, yet the captain continued to gun the boat as though it were gliding on a glassy pond. Worse, someone had neglected to tie the bowline, which somehow uncurled under the boat and caught in the propellers of the two outboards. At 12:30 P.M. the boat stopped abruptly and dove like a missile into the trough of a wave. The glacially cold water washed in, and the boat almost went over—in the middle of the 250-foot deep lake. If the vessel swamped here, everyone would become hypothermic in a matter of seconds; in a few more minutes, death would seize the entire group. Instead the boat pitched in the high seas for the next few hours.

Both outboards were shot, and there were no backups. Several times the boat almost capsized, but finally it drifted close to the southeastern shore, where Peter Metz, an escort for the Antarctica group, heroically leapt into the water, fully clothed with rope in hand, and swam to the jagged shore. There he managed to secure the line, and as the boat crashed against a shoreline cliff, he and Arian helped the passengers to shore. At 9:30 P.M., nine hours after the ordeal began, the last passenger staggered into the explora, en Patagonia lodge. "I will never go on a boat in Lago Grey again," Arian announced at the end of his tale. I believed him, but was a bit surprised by the severe reaction. Afterall, this was the wilderness, and by definition, the only thing predictable is that the unpredictable will happen, and the only adventure is the well-planned itinerary gone wrong.

It was after dark when we arrived in Torres del Paine National Park, and as I got out of the van I met the frigid, fire-hose-force wind for which Patagonia is famous. It slapped my face, stung my hands, and I had to bend to a 45° angle to walk. Several months ago I had figured I'd spent about a quarter of my nights as an adult in a sleeping bag, and had always assumed I would do the same when I came to Patagonia. But now, as I slipped

LAGO PEHUE, A GLACIAL LAKE THE COLOR OF A TROPICAL LAGOON, SET AGAINST THE BACKDROP OF LOS CUERNOS DEL PAINE, THE ANGULAR GREY AND BLACK HORNS THAT ARE EMBLEMATIC OF THE PARK AND THE REGION.

THIS IS A LAND OF WIND-
WHIPPED LAKES,
BILLOWING SKIES,
ROLLING HILLS, AND
SHARP MOUNTAINS.

through the double doors of the explora, en Patagonia lodge, I was happy I wasn't setting up a tent. And as I entered the lobby, it was like being dropped into Oz by a tornado.

The explora, en Patagonia, just three months old, was a marvel. Warm, clean, and luxurious, its panels were all hand-tooled and carefully polished. In the hall, smooth curved walls emitted a delicate cypress scent. Though there are just thirty rooms in this lodge, there were forty staff members on hand, and one immediately led me down a Swiss sisal carpet to a carafe of rich Chilean red wine waiting alongside pickled partridge, pork terrine, and grilled lamb, all presented on British porcelain. The buffet offered scallops mousse, pastel do choclos (Chilean chicken-corn casserole), corvina fish with tarragon sauce, salmon carpaccio, baked rabbit, stuffed artichokes, Roquefort-spinach ravioli, and papayas stuffed with kiwi. This was a far cry from my usual freeze-dried camping fare. After dinner, I collapsed on a sofa bed plumped up with a white pique bedspread, goose-down pillows, and crisp cotton sheets from Barcelona. It reminded me that my sleeping bag was long overdue for a drycleaning.

But it was morning that made the biggest impression. I awoke to a choice summer day, and the finest bedroom view I had ever seen: an unobstructed vista of Lago Pehue, a lake the color of a tropical lagoon; of Los Cuernos del Paine, the angular gray and black Paine Horns, sculpted by twelve million years of ice and wind; and the Torres del Paine, the vertical spires after which the park is named. The hotel's architects, Germand del Sol and Jose Cruz, had also cleverly cut a hole through the bathroom wall, so I could relax in the jacuzzi bath or sit on the loo and be regaled by the needles of granite piercing the icy sky.

The view was so compelling I was late to meet my guide for the day, Alejandra Manalla. She was waiting in front of the giant fireplace in the lobby, and something about her struck me immediately. She wore glasses and was tall, thin as a camel's neck, a bit gangly, and had big lanternlike eyes. She was eighteen and a half years old (her emphasis on the half), and working as a guide during her summer away from college, where she was studying to be a writer.

Pablo Neruda, the great Chilean poet, was an inspiration to her, and I told her he had influenced me as well. In fact, I had made a pilgrimage to his house in Santiago just a few days ago. As we discussed this, we were traveling down the road to Guarderia Lago Sarmiento, and during one bump I suddenly recognized something . . . she reminded me of me. At eighteen and a half I, too, had just become a guide, was studying writing, and was tall, spectacled, lanky, and quite unsure of myself. She seemed more confident than I was my first season, until I asked her about a series of scratches and wounds on her hand and wrist. She turned pale, then told me she had scratched herself while hiking through a tangle of calafate plants. But red abrasions belied that explanation, so I asked again. She hesitated, then revealed she had gotten hurt

THE GUANACO IS THE WILD COUSIN OF THE LLAMA. AS A RESULT OF PRESERVATION EFFORTS, NOW AN ESTIMATED 3,000 GUANACOS ROAM FREELY IN THE SHADOW OF THE TORRES DEL PAINE.

trying to climb from the boat in Lago Grey as it crashed against the cliff. She went on to describe her version of the previous Sunday's events. Still very much the apprentice and without much to do she had nodded off before the boat first crashed into the trough, but then found herself thrust into the role of guide. She did all she could to keep the clients calm, though she was more scared than she had ever been, and thought she was going to die. When she finished her account she looked at me and said with some authority, "I will never go on a boat in Grey Lake again. Never."

As if to punctuate Alejandra's conclusion, a furry, caramel-colored, abbreviated version of a giraffe skipped across the road on spindly legs: it was a guanaco, the wild cousin of the llama. I was excited and asked if we could stop to take a photo, but Alejandra insisted I be patient. She told me male guanacos like to surround themselves with harems, and there would be greater numbers ahead. She was right, of course. A few minutes later we passed a knot of three guanacos, then a dozen, then a herd of twenty or more. Suddenly, they were everywhere, like 250-pound gremlins. Occasionally, one would stare directly at me with its long lashes and Bette Davis eyes; I was enchanted by them.

At Guarderoa Lago Sarmiento, we exited the van and started to hike among the guanacos. We walked north, toward Guarderia Y Refugio Laguna Amarga, following a wire fence separating the park from an *estancia* (a large ranch). Every now and then we'd find a cinnamon-colored tulango, a baby guanaco, caught in the wire, formless as a pricked balloon, yet stiff with rigor mortis. The fence seemed an inhumane intrusion, until Alejandra explained that just a few years ago there were less than 300 gunancos left in the region. The ranchers in the area had shot the guancos, who overgrazed their sheep ranchland. But with the establishment of Torres del Paine National Park, fences were erected, and the population within has swelled. Now an estimated 3,000 guanacos roam freely in the shadow of the Torres del Paine.

At one point I lagged behind our group, trying to photograph the silhouette of a woolly guanaco against the palatial cluster of ice-clad peaks and granite teeth. Then a Patagonian red fox waved his glossy tail in the tall grass just a few feet from my camera, and I lightly stepped over for a closer look. I was so close I could feel hot breath before it scampered away. Where else, I wondered, did wild animals grow up with such an underwhelming fear of man?

After the fox trotted, I heard a tremulous cry from up on the hill. It was Alejandra, calling me to catch up with the group. Her voice sounded tentative, missing the authority I associated with guides. But it was effective. I stashed my camera and hurried to catch up. When I arrived I told Alejandra a story about how I had been in a capsize of a raft on a river in Africa in 1973. I had been the oarsman. I made a misjudgment, and a man drowned. I was so devastated by the accident I swore to give up guiding, and I did, for a long year. But finally, the art of the wilds I so enjoyed while guiding overwhelmed the carpings of reason, and I stepped back onto a raft. And I found a resonance in the river that had never rung before. Alejandra just looked at me with her big eyes.

As the oblique, orange light of evening bathed the celebrated towers, I returned to the explora, en Patagonia, where I met Peter and Shirley Metz, the escorts for the Antarctica group that had taken the ill-fated cruise across Lago Grey. Peter was the hero in the epic; while the Chilian crew panicked, he kept a cool head and

ESTABLISHED IN 1959, THIS IS THE CROWN JEWEL OF CHILE'S MANY GORGEOUS NATIONAL PARKS.

kept the others calm. It wasn't the first time Peter had acted the hero. He was on the tarmac in Puerto Williams in February 1991, when a chartered LAN-Chile British Aerospace 146, carrying a group of Antarctica-bound tourists, overshot the runway and crashed into the Beagle Channel. Peter was in the plane in minutes, pulling out survivors and bodies. Of the seventy-two on board, nineteen died. And when a Society Expeditions Zodiac capsized in the Tuamotus of French Polynesia, killing two, Peter was there, and helped get the survivors to shore. It appeared Peter possessed an Homeric catalogue of heroism, but he was also earning a grim reputation for attracting disasters. Over a salad I asked Peter about the Lago Grey incident. He didn't want to talk about it. "But," I protested, "there are lessons here. You did the right things. Others didn't. Don't you think we could all learn by hearing about this?"

"No. I don't believe anything good can come from talking about such an incident. It would only give more people pause before visiting this region. It would be bad for busi-

MALE GUANACOS LIKE TO SURROUND THEM- SELVES WITH HAREMS AND CAN BE LIKENED TO 250-POUND GREMLINS WITH BETTE DAVIS EYES.

ness." I noticed then there was more than a soupçon of vinegar in the salad dressing. And even though we talked and drank deep into the evening, Peter never altered his perspective. And I didn't regret that Peter wouldn't be joining me for the rest of my exploration.

The following day I began hiking up to the base of the Torres del Paine with Arian, Alejandra, and several hotel guests. These would be my first steps into the Cordillera del Paine, the 30-mile-long range adjacent to but geographically separate from the Andes. Like Yosemite, the Paine range was shaped by glacial action during the Pleistocene epoch. In geological terms it is an upthrusted batholith, a gigantic bubble of once-molten granite that rose from the center of the earth, and was later covered with huge glaciers stretching from the continental ice cap. When the glaciers retreated, they left behind deep gashes in the "bubble," and an uproar of wild peaks that rise from the grassy lowlands near sea level.

It was an odd but satisfying hike as we followed the south bank of the cascading Rio Ascensio upwards, across bogs of primordial muck where Alejandra's tiny feet left an impression the size of a bear paw. The name Patagonia was not meant to designate a political unity but a land of big-footed Indians, the *Patagones*, as Antonia Pigafetta, chron- icler of Ferdinand Magellan's 1520 voyage, named them when he found giant prints near

THE TOWERS OF PAINE ARE SURROUNDED BY STRINGS OF MANY LARGE AND SMALL
LAKES IN DIFFERENT SHAPES AND COLOR, VARYING FROM BRIGHT BLUE TO
TURQUOISE GREEN AND PALE GREY.

their winter camp. I couldn't help but wonder if the mud here may have been the cause of those first impressions, and ultimately the name for a fifth of a continent.

Arian bounced between the four women clients, but Alejandra kept pace with me, interpreting the natural history, pointing out the hundred-year-old lenga trees, the gnarled Magellanic beeches, the pale tresses of old man's beard, and the mountain guanaco, while nodding her head at Arian and his flirtations. "Mountain guanaco?" I played the straight man, while dumbly staring at the knot of women being entertained by a very handsome and confident guide. "That's Arian. He always has a harem." Her smile was as bright as a phosphorus fire. Even though this was just her second hike up this path, it was evident Alejandra knew a lot. She loved what she was doing, and confessed she couldn't believe how lucky she was to have this job. In some archaeological way, I remembered the same feeling.

After crawling over the crest of a steep scree slope, I lifted my eyes to a sky full of mountains: Torre Nord (7,400 feet), Torre Sur (8,200 feet), and Torre Central (8,100 feet). They looked like colossal crystals growing side-by-side just across a small alpine lake set in a snow-streaked cirque. The microclimates of Patagonia showed their mercurial colors, with one moment bright and sunshiny, the next dark and blustery, the striated spires perforating boiling deep gray clouds. I took several photos of Alejandra, who seemed lofty as her backdrop. Her eyes seemed to reflect all the wonder of a new world.

Saturday I signed up for a horseback ride. I had expected Arian, but he took the day off, pleading neurasthenia. This time my guide was Giovanna Raineri, twenty-three, from Santiago. She had worked the year before in the Chile Pavilion at the Universal Exposition in Seville, and there met the owners of explora, who invited her to join the staff as a guide. She had the adamantine look of an outdoorswoman, and exuded confidence as we rode along the lapis-tinted Paine River. We passed wind-twisted trees, zigzagging *nandues* (flightless ostrich-like birds, also known as Darwin rheas), *liebres* (European hares), a *cingue* (Patagonian skunk), and a sparkling spring, where the water tasted like swamp juice. At one point I asked Giovanna if she had been in the notorious boat, and a panicked look sped across her face. "Yes, I was there," she said. "It was the most frightening episode of my life. I will never step on a boat on Lago Grey again." Then she kicked her heels into the side of her steed and galloped ahead.

At lunch, over a Magallanes-style lamb and vegetable barbecue cooked over glowing beechwood coals, Alejandra showed up at the *quincho* to help. After a couple of pisco sours, I asked if she would join us for the afternoon ride. She said she didn't really know how to ride, but sure, she would love to. After a quick lesson Alejandra was in the saddle and trotting beside me. We rode to a small waterfall, and scrambled up some slippery rocks to a ledge above the main pool. Alejandra told me that just a few days before, the explora's chief driver, Pedro, "The Silver Fox," had jumped into the pool, not knowing how to swim. He flailed around for a bit, but made it to shore, and emerged smiling. Alejandra seemed impressed, as though through witnessing Pedro's spirited response to

THE PAINE MOUNTAINS ARE A DISTINCT RANGE OF PEAKS CONNECTED TO THE MAIN
ANDEAN CHAIN BY A MOUNTAIN PASS, THE PASO PAINE. THE RANGE RUNS IN A
WEST-TO-EAST DIRECTION, AS OPPOSED TO THE ANDES' NORTH-SOUTH AXIS.
THE LENGTH, SLIGHTLY LESS THAN THIRTY MILES, MAKES IT A COMPACT AND
EASILY ACCESSIBLE RANGE.

misadventure something stirred within her, seemingly in collaboration with the forces at the bottom of the world.

The following day, we made arrangements to visit the Valle del Frances, an enclosed sanctuary deeply incised into the Cordillera del Paine. In order to get there we would have to take a boat across Lago Pehue; then we would ride horses for several miles, to the Italian Camp, and finally hike the final pitch to the foot of the French Glacier. I had hoped Alejandra would come along, but she wasn't in the lobby, and I wondered if it was just too soon for her to cross another lake. This time my guide was Pepe Alarcon. Of course, I expected to hear his personal reactions to the boating accident. As we loaded the launch, I asked Pepe about the incident. He turned to me and said he had no reaction . . . he wasn't there. In fact, he was in the hotel explora, en Patagonia helping to coordinate the rescue by radio.

Just as the outboards kicked, Alejandra came running down the pier and jumped on board. She was barely breathing through her crinkly smile, despite the hundred-yard dash, and I admired the streamlined fitness of her youth. When I told her she was fortunate to be young and in such good shape, she looked back at me intently and said, "But you know, I really like wrinkles." I felt like a turtle with its shell off.

The crossing was easy. Someone had turned the Patagonian fan off and the lake, which has no fish, was flat as a griddle. Soon we were saddled up and loping our way into the mountains. This time Alejandra seemed at home on her horse. She trotted ahead, leaving me in the rear but always looking back to check my progress. We parked our horses at the Italian camp, enjoyed a picnic lunch, then took off by foot to reach the high vantage. As we arrived at the crest of the walk, a lime-green *cachana* (Austral parakeet) zipped over my shoulder, and the mountain began to tremble. If the flap of a butterfly's wing in Osaka can affect the weather in Kansas, imagine what a parakeet can do in the beefy wind of Patagonia. The bird may or may not have contributed, but several thunderous noises boomed across the valley. I turned my head and watched a series of avalanches spill from the upper reaches of the French Glacier, which flows from the Paine Grande Massif (10,600 feet), the highest point in the Paine fretwork. The glacier itself was a spectacular mass of ice and snow, splintered with deep canyons and jagged pinnacles, a bristling blue. I turned again and looked up into the smooth-walled Gothic Towers; another quarter turn and I looked down on the pearl-colored waters of Lake Nordenskjold. It was all savagely beautiful.

On the way back a williwaw hit, and the portrait of sharp relief we'd enjoyed on the ride up was now a canvas of grey vagueness. I slouched in my poncho like Lee Marvin in *Cat Ballou*, bringing up the rear, sometimes getting lost. I'd call out Alejandra's name, but the wind would suck it up and toss it with the rain toward the Towers behind me. Wrapped in clouds, they now looked bent, like huge mourners at a funeral. Then I would see an orange blaze painted on a tree or rock, and I'd be back on track.

Once we got to the shores of Lago Pehue the wind cranked up its battering, the rain its lashing. Whitecaps whipped across the lake. Several Andean condors, the world's largest flying birds, traced curves across the leaden sky. We boarded the boat and began the forty-five-minute crossing. As we plunged through the gray-green swells, the boat pitched and reeled. Alejandra sat across from me, looking stern despite her youth, and deep in thought. At one point, her face lifted like a balloon, her eyes dark but bright, and with a weatherburned smile she said, "You know, I think I *would* go back on a boat on Lago Grey." And I know then that somewhere in the mountain landscape of this woman there was a magic glass into which she stepped as a human, and came out a guide.

EPILOGUE

After wandering among plateaus and peaks for what seemed like an epoch, we felt we had perhaps found higher ground. Then again, we weren't quite sure; a tiny pouch of emptiness still hung from our belts. So it was that at the end of these journeys we found ourselves reflecting on the beginnings.

Long before we sought the landscapes described in these pages, we had started our rambles up mountains. But though we always started up the path united, for many years we never reached a summit together. In Sri Lanka, on Adams Peak, we each stepped to the zenith separately, months apart. On Lombok we climbed to within 1,000 feet of the 12,000-foot-high rim of the volcano Rinjani, but turned back. In the Rockies and Sierras we hiked and camped, but never bagged a peak. In Tasmania, I continued up Frenchman's Cap as Pamela set up camp; it was the same at the Great Smokey Mountain in Bahrain.

It wasn't until 1992 that we both reached a mountain summit together. It was Gunung Batur, a holy peak in the highlands of Bali. It was just a one-day ascent up the mile-high volcano, mostly scrambling up the hard black debris of recent eruptions. On top we stared into the belly of the beast, the dark caldera and sipped cold sodas, purchased from some entrepreneur who had set up a refreshment stand on the crater rim. This little expedition had been planned spontaneously, with no work, no quest in mind, and as such Pamela had not brought a camera, nor I a pen. We had nothing to do with our hands on top, so we held hands, and began the long descent.

After reaching the village of Purajati we climbed into a *bemo*, a local taxi, and began winding down the rest of the mountain. At one point the driver stopped for tea in a pre-Hindu village, and as we sat under a banana tree, an ethereal music began to waft into our ears. It was the *gamelan*, the ancient breath of Indonesia. The land seemed to bend with the loose, rainlike melody, to soften as its edges washed away.

Our driver cocked his ear, smiled, and told us this was the music of Dewi Sri, the beautiful goddess of rice and fertility. He then pointed to a palm-leaf wall-hanging depicting an abstract female head with a large, fanlike headdress: an effigy of Dewi Sri, he said. Beneath the hanging was an offering, a small bowl filled with flowers, rice, and eggs, to discourage evil spirits from taking away the seeds. When Dewi Sri came to this village, our driver told us in a conspiratorial way, she would sing her song and the rice would ripen. And young women in the village would complain of a fullness in their bellies. We humored our host with a smile, finished our tea, and headed downhill to the beach.

Now, several years later, with our project completed, we rested, and thought about things yet undone, about things we wished we had done, but now never would. Then a call came from our friends at Garuda, the national airline of Indonesia. They were having a party in San Francisco, and would we attend? We accepted with alacrity.

As we sat among friends and tables blooming with flowers, we ate *sate, mie goreng,* and dishes made from rice and eggs. A child with a large fanlike headdress emerged from behind a curtain to perform a dance. And a gamelan orchestra began to play its free and flighty sounds. It was the same music we had heard on the side of Gunung Batur, the song of Dewi Sri, and it seemed to penetrate our souls like water soaks into a field.

As we walked across the room at the end of the evening, we saw a photograph on the wall. We stopped for a moment to drink in its image: in the distance a mountain peak was wreathed in clouds, in the foreground a green curtain of terraced fields were sprouting with rice. Then we continued to the car. Halfway home Pamela told me she felt a stirring in her belly. And for the first time in our wanderings, we felt whole. And it was the miracle of the mountains we thanked.